ID0946782

Great Passenger Ships of the World

Volume 6: 1977–1986

Great Passenger Ships of the World

Volume 6: 1977–1986

Arnold Kludas

Translated by Keith Lewis

Patrick Stephens, Wellingborough

© Copyright 1984 Koehlers Verlagsgesellschaft mbH, Herford.
© Copyright 1986 Patrick Stephens Limited

All rights reserved. No part of this publication may be reproduced, stored in a retrieval system or transmitted, in any form or by any means, electronic, mechanical, photocopying, recording or otherwise, without prior permission in writing from the publishers.

First published in Germany under the title *Die Grossen Passagierschiffe Fähren und Cruise Liner der Welt*
First published in Great Britain—1986
Reprinted January 1987

Kludas, Arnold
[Die grossen Passagierschiffe de Welt]. Great passenger ships of the world.
Vol. 6, 1977-1986
1. Passenger ships—History—Pictorial works
I. [Die grossen Passagierschiffe de Welt]
II. Title
387.2'43'09034   VM381

ISBN 0-85059-747-1

Patrick Stephens Limited is part of the Thorsons Publishing Group

Printed and bound in Great Britain.

Foreword

It is now 12 years since the appearance of the final volume of the original German edition of my Great Passenger Ships of the World. *In 1976 a second and expanded printing was published which was followed between 1974 and 1976 by an English translation wherein material was further updated. However, even this did not enable me to keep pace with the continuous stream of changes. For a long time a supplement was planned which would not only bring the ships' careers up to date but would also include those vessels which had entered service during the intervening years. Since the publication of the most recent edition a number of new passenger ships with a tonnage in excess of 10,000 have been completed. On the other hand, many then in service no longer exist by reason of casualty or sale to breakers, while others are still afloat but have had their passenger accommodation removed, or been renamed, or now sail for different owners. Some, following changes of flag, have been remeasured to gross tonnages below 10,000. These manipulations of tonnage have in recent years put obstacles in my way, but all ships laid down since 18 July 1982 have to be measured in accordance with a universal system of tonnage calculation, and by 1995 this will have to be adopted for older vessels still afloat. It will not then be possible, for instance, for Home Line's* Atlantic, *having dimensions similar to those of Hapag-Lloyd's* Europa, *to be more than a third less in size in terms of gross tonnage.*

Among new ships covered in this book ferries form a major element, their tremendous development since the 1970s having been breathtaking. In the Baltic today there are ferries of 36,000 gross tons with a capacity for 2,500 passengers and 580 cars. In addition the accommodation aboard these modern ferries has reached a remarkably high standard. However, the largest and most comfortable passenger vessels are, of course, the cruise liners, many dating from the early 1970s having since been lengthened. New ships have for a long time exceeded 30,000 gross tons and ships of 45,000 have been commissioned. Notwithstanding international economic crises the cruising market shows no sign of recession, and in fact continues to grow.

In compiling this volume I have once again had the invaluable and willing help of friends in all parts of the world. Above all I should like to thank my many readers for their encouraging letters and calls, not least for the stimulus they gave me. I am particularly happy to thank those people around the world who have supplied many of the illustrations contained within these pages. Without their prompt and considerate assistance production of a book like this would have been quite impossible. In conclusion I gratefully acknowledge the translator, Keith Lewis. Since this English edition has been published three years after the German original, there proved to be much supplementary information to be incorporated. Mr Lewis has therefore done more than simply translate and I have enjoyed our friendly co-operation.

Arnold Kludas
Bremerhaven: January 1986

Explanatory Notes

The present work is a continuation of the five-volume *Great Passenger Ships of the World,* up-dating the series first published between 1975 and 1977, and reprinted between 1984 and 1986. It covers all passenger ships and ferries measured at 10,000 gross tons and over, existing—or under construction—in 1986. At the same time the form of the ship-biographies and classification of material has been modified compared with what was contained in the earlier volumes.

In the main part of the book passenger ships and ferries in service during 1986 are given their present names followed where applicable by former names. The sequence is that of launching date with sister ships, irrespective of chronological order, covered immediately after the name-ship of a class. Ships which have become 10,000-tonners and over consequent upon rebuilding are entered from the dates of their having come into service with such measurement.

Appendix 1 traces the later careers of ships included in the first five volumes of *Great Passenger Ships of the World* which still existed in 1986 but were either no longer seagoing passenger-carriers or had been remeasured to a gross tonnage below 10,000.

Appendix 2 finalises the stories of ships dealt with in the above five-volume work which, between 1976 and 1986, have been either broken up or become total loss casualties. For clarity, repetition in Appendices 1 and 2 of complete biographies has had to be foregone. Only variations since 1976 are entered.

In most cases technical details have been taken from Lloyd's Register of Shipping. In the case of new or projected ships not yet appearing in the Register, reference has been made to technical publications and information released by the respective shipyards. Historical data mirrors in chronological order the life of each ship, noting all the important events in her career. Where a ship has been rebuilt, revised technical details follow the date of completion of the work. Subsequent changes of a technical

nature are noted against applicable dates.

When no final disposal is noted, the ship is still in service under the stated name at the date of going to press (June 1986). Also at this time it may not have been possible to obtain full details for every new ship, but all the information in this book is as up to date as possible at the time of going to press.

The following is a guide to the technical and historical information concerning the ships.

I. Technical Data

The information given in the paragraph on technical data is as up-to-date as possible at the time of writing. Planned specifications are given in the case of incompleted ships for which at their respective stages of construction these had not been fully decided upon. Alterations affecting technical data are noted with historical notes against the appropriate dates.

Tonnage Given as gross registered tonnage (GRT) and deadweight tonnage (DWT).

Dimensions Length over all × moulded breadth in metres (m) rounded off to one place of decimals, followed by the equivalent in feet (ft), the length to the nearest whole number and breadth to one place of decimals. Length overall has been adopted in preference to other length measurements. It was found that recorded registered length and length between perpendiculars could vary from time to time and from place to place.

Propulsion Type of machinery, constructor. Where the shipbuilder has not been responsible for the propelling machinery, its constructor is given. Triple exp denotes triple expansion engines, cyl denotes cylinders, and kW denotes kilowatts.

Power The figure of horse power given is the highest performance attainable by the engines in normal service. The

different methods of measuring horse power, according to the form of propulsion, are as follows:
IHP = indicated horse power, unit of measurement for reciprocating steam engines and internal combustion engines.
SHP = shaft horse power, unit of measurement for turbine machinery and internal combustion engines.
BHP = brake horse power, unit of measurement for internal combustion engines.

The horse power figures, thus arrived at through different methods, cannot necessarily be compared with each other. While BHP and SHP are practically identical, their relationship to the indicated horse power (IHP) is in the region of 4:5. 8,000 SHP is thus equivalent to 10,000 IHP.

Speed Service speed is given in knots (kn). This is followed, as far as can be established, by the highest speed achieved on trials with the engines running at maximum power.

Passengers On nearly all ships the passenger accommodation and the number of berths for each class are frequently altered. The information on alterations to passenger accommodation therefore is limited to really significant modifications, as far as it has been possible to determine them.

Crew Changes in crew-strength have not always been noted. Unfortunately it has not been possible even to determine the initial crew-strength for every ship.

II. Historical Data

The historical information reflects in chronological order the career of the ship, giving all important events and facts.

Owners In the ships' biographies, shipowners are indicated throughout in full style as recorded in Lloyd's Register. It is assumed that Cie, Cia, AG, SA, etc, will be as familiar to readers as are such English

Contents

abbreviations as SN, Co, Corp, etc.
Details are also given of each ship's
port of registry (abbreviated as PoR),
which is not necessarily where the
shipowner has his head office.

Builders Like shipowners, builders are
noted throughout in full style as
recorded in Lloyd's Register.

Completion Completion-date is the
date of commencement of trials.

Steamer *Admiral Nakhimov*
Black Sea Shipping Co, Odessa
PoR: Odessa

Ex *Berlin*

Builders: Bremer Vulkan
Schiffbau & Maschinenfabrik,
Vegesack
Yard no: 614
17,053 GRT; 8,942 DWT; 174.3 ×
21.0 m / 572 × 68.9 ft; Two 4-cyl
triple exp engines from builders;
Twin screw; 9,000 kW (12,000
IHP); 16 kn; Passengers: 870.

1925 Mar 24: Launched as *Berlin*
for Norddeutscher Lloyd,
Bremen.
Sep 17: Delivered. 15,286 GRT.
Passengers: 220 1st class, 284 2nd
class, 618 3rd class. Crew: 326.

Sep 26: Maiden voyage
Bremerhaven-New York.
1928 Nov 13: *Berlin* rescued 23
survivors from British passenger
steamer *Vestris* which had sunk in
Atlantic storm on previous day.
1929 Passengers: 257 cabin class,
261 tourist class, 361 3rd class.
1938 Oct: Laid up at
Bremerhaven.
1939 Chartered by 'Kraft durch
Freude' ('Strength through Joy')
for two cruises.
Jul 17: Boiler explosion shortly
before she reached port on voyage
to Swinemünde, where she was to
have been taken up for service
with German Navy. 17 of crew
killed.
Aug 23: Converted at Hamburg
for service as hospital ship.

1945 During night of Jan 31-Feb 1
struck a mine off Swinemünde.
Struck a second mine while
attempts were being made to tow
her to shallow water and sank.
1949 Raised by Soviet salvors.
Renamed *Admiral Nakhimov*.
Repaired and refitted at Warnow
yard, Warnemünde.
1957 May: Handed over to Soviet
state shipping line. Has since
operated mainly in Black Sea but
also made Transatlantic voyages
to Cuba.
1986 Sep 1: Sank in Black Sea
following collision with *Pyotr
Vasev*. 398 dead.

1 *Certainly the most senior among the
world's great passenger ships, the
Soviet* Admiral Nakhimov, *ex* Berlin.
(Kludas collection.)

1

Turbine steamer *Britanis*
Ajax Navigation Corp (D.
Chandris), Panama
PoR: Panama

Ex *Lurline*
Ex *Matsonia*
Ex *Monterey*

Builders: Bethlehem Shipbuilding
Corp Ltd, Quincy/Mass
Yard no: 1441
18,153 GRT; 4,264 DWT; 192.5 ×
24.1 m / 631 × 79.1 ft; Two sets
geared turbines from builders;
Twin screw; 18,650 kW (25,000
SHP); 21.5 kn; Passengers: 1,632;
Crew: approx 350.

1931 Oct 10: Launched as
Monterey for Matson Navigation
Co, San Francisco.
1932 Apr 20: Delivered. 18,017
GRT. Passengers: 472 1st class,
229 cabin class.
May 12: Maiden voyage San
Francisco-Honolulu-Sydney.
1941 Dec: US Army troop
transport.
1946 Dec 26: Returned to Matson.
Refit at Alameda halted for
financial reasons.

1952 Sold to US Government.
Laid up in Suisun Bay.
1956 Feb 3: Repurchased by
Matson.
Apr: Refit and modernisation at
Newport News until May 1957.
Renamed *Matsonia*.
1957 May 17: 18,655 GRT.
Passengers: 761 1st class.
May 22: First voyage New York-
Los Angeles, then old route San
Francisco-Los Angeles-Honolulu.
1963 Dec 6: Renamed *Lurline*.
1970 Jun 30: Sold to Chandris,
Piraeus. Refitted at Piraeus.
Renamed *Britanis*. 18,254 GRT.

1971 Feb 21: First voyage, round-
the-world service, Southampton-
Sydney-Southampton.
1975 Cruising only.
1982 May: Chartered by Fantasy
Cruises, New York, for cruising
between New York and Bermuda.
Registered in Panama. 18,153
GRT.
1985 One day cruises from New
York.

Turbine steamer *Ellinis*
Australia Line SA (D. Chandris),
Panama
PoR: Piraeus

Ex *Lurline*

Builders: Bethlehem Shipbuilding
Corp Ltd, Quincy/Mass
Yard no: 1447
18,564 GRT; 10,389 DWT; 192.5
× 24.1 m / 632 × 79.1 ft; Two
sets geared turbines from builders;
Twin screw; 18,650 kW (25,000
SHP); 19.5 kn; Passengers: 1,398;
Crew: approx 350.

1932 Jul 18: Launched as *Lurline*
for Matson Navigation Co, San
Francisco.
Dec: Completed. 18,021 GRT;
Passengers: 550 1st class, 250
cabin class; Crew: 360.
1933 Jan 27: Maiden voyage,
round-the-world cruise from San
Francisco. Regular service, San
Francisco-Honolulu.
1941 Dec 11: Taken over by US
War Shipping Administration as
US Navy transport. 18,163 GRT.
1946 May 29: Returned to Matson.
Overhaul and refit at Alameda to
1948. 18,564 GRT.
1948 Apr 15: San Francisco-Los
Angeles-Honolulu service.

1963 Sep: Sold to Dimitri
Chandris and refitted by Smith's
Dock Co Ltd, North Shields.
Renamed *Ellinis*.
Dec 30: First voyage Piraeus-
Sydney.
1964 Round-the-world service
Rotterdam-Sydney-Rotterdam.
1974 Jul 25: Turbine damage at
Rotterdam. Affected installation
was replaced by one from broken
up sister ship *Homeric*.
1975 Cruising only.
1980 Oct 14: Laid up at Piraeus.
1986 Nov: Sold Liberian-flag
interests.

1 *The world's oldest cruise liner still in
service. As the* Monterey, *the
Britannis was built as long ago as
1932.* (Alex Duncan.)
2 *Laid up at Piraeus since 1980, the
future of the* Ellinis *is doubtful.*
(Kludas collection.)

1

2

Motorship *The Victoria*
Phaidon Navigation SA, Panama
(Chandris Group)
PoR: Panama

Ex *Victoria*
Ex *Dunnottar Castle*

Builders: Harland & Wolff Ltd,
Belfast
Yard no: 959
14,411 GRT; 6,590 DWT; 173.5 ×
21.8 m / 569 × 71.5 ft; Two 7-cyl
diesels, FIAT; Twin screw; 10,450
kW (14,000 BHP); 16 kn;
Passengers: 500.

1936 Jan 25: Launched as
Dunnottar Castle for Union-
Castle Mail Steamship Co Ltd,
London.
Jun: Completed. 15,007 GRT;
Length overall: 170.7 m / 560 ft;
Diesels, Burmeister & Wain-
Harland & Wolff; 11,200 BHP; 17
kn; Passengers: 258 1st class, 250
tourist class.
Jul: Maiden voyage Southampton-

Cape Town. Then London-round
Africa service.
1939 Oct 14: Armed merchant
cruiser.
1942 Troop transport.
1948 Released from war service.
Following overhaul, 15,054 GRT.
Passengers: 105 1st class, 263
tourist class.
1949 Feb: First postwar voyage in
civilian service, London-round
Africa.
1958 Sold to Incres Steamship Co
Ltd, Monrovia.
1959 Renamed *Victoria*.
Jan: Arrived at Wilton-Fijenoord
yard, Rotterdam, for conversion
to cruise liner to carry 600
passengers. 14,917 GRT; Length
overall 174.4 m / 572 ft; New
FIAT diesels fitted giving 16,800
BHP; Service speed 18 kn,
maximum 21 kn.
Dec 14: Rotterdam-Southampton
and short Mediterranean cruise.
1960 Jan 8: Positioning voyage Le
Havre-New York, then cruising

New York-West Indies.
1964 Oct: Sold to Victoria
Steamship Co Ltd, Monrovia,
subsidiary of Rederi A/B Clipper
(Einar Hansen), Malmö, Sweden.
Continued cruising to Caribbean.
1975 Nov: Sold to Phaidon
Navigation Co, Panama, part of
Chandris group.
Dec 11: Arrived at Piraeus in tow
of *Heidi Moran*.
1977 Renamed *The Victoria*.
1978 11,886 GRT.
1981 Sold to Victoria Maritime
Corp, Monrovia. Cruising in
European and Caribbean waters.
1984 Sold back to Phaidon
Navigation SA, Panama. 14,411
GRT.

1 The Victoria, *yet another veteran
from the 1930s.* (Kludas collection.)
2 The *Emerald Seas, a former P 2
troop transport, photographed at
Miami on 24 December 1982.* (Martin
Lochte-Holtgreven.)

Turbine steamer *Emerald Seas*
Eastern Steamship Lines Inc,
Panama
PoR: Panama

Ex *Atlantis*
Ex *President Roosevelt*
Ex *Leilani*
Ex *La Guardia*
Ex *General W. P. Richardson*

Builders: Federal Shipbuilding &
Dry Dock Co, Kearny, NJ
Yard no: 276
18,936 GRT; 189.8 × 23.0 m /
623 × 75.5 ft; Two sets geared
turbines, De Laval; Twin screw;
14,000 kW (18,700 SHP); 19 kn;
Passengers: 920.

1944 Aug 6: Launched as *General
W.P. Richardson* for US Navy.
Until April 1944 intended name
had been *General R.M.Blatchford*.
Oct 31: Delivered. 17,811 GRT.
Accommodation for 5,200 men.
Nov 2: Commissioned. Number:
AP 118.

Dec 10: Maiden voyage Boston-
Southampton.
1946 Feb 14: Transferred to US
Army.
1948 Mar 10: Laid up.
Chartered by American Export
Lines Inc. Rebuilt at Pascagoula
for civilian passenger service.
Renamed *La Guardia*. Passengers:
157 1st class, 452 tourist class.
1949 May 27: First voyage New
York-Genoa. From October, to
Haifa.
1951 Dec 13: Transferred to US
Maritime Commission. Laid up in
James River.
1955 Sold to Hawaiian Steamship
Co, Textron Inc, New York.
18,298 GRT following refit.
1956 Jul: Renamed *Leilani*.
California-Hawaii service.
1958 Textron Inc went bankrupt.
Dec 29: *Leilani* laid up.
1959 Jun: Offered at auction by
Maritime Administration.
1960 Sold to American President
Lines Ltd, San Francisco.

1961 Mar 1: Work commenced at
Seattle on conversion to luxury
liner by Puget Sound Bridge &
Dredging Co.
Renamed *President Roosevelt*.
1962 Apr 16: Commissioned.
18,920 GRT. Passengers: 456 1st
class.
May 10: First voyage San
Francisco-Yokohama.
1970 Sold to D & A Chandris.
Registered under ownership of
Solon Navegacion SA, Piraeus.
Converted at Perama for cruising.
Renamed *Atlantis*.
1971 Jun: 24,458 GRT. Passengers:
756 in one class, maximum 1,092.
Cruising from US ports.
1972 Oct: Sold to Ares Shipping
Corp, Monrovia. Renamed
Emerald Seas. Continued cruising
from US ports. 18,936 GRT.
1984 Transferred to Eastern
Steamship Lines Inc, Panama
(Gotaas-Larsen Shipping Corp).
1986 Jul 31: Fire while off Nassau
— 17 injured.

2

Turbine steamer *Aquarama*
Sand Products Corp, Detroit, Mich
PoR: Wilmington

Ex Marine Star

Builders: Sun Shipbuilding & Dry Dock Co, Chester, Pa
Yard no: 357
12,773 GRT; 151.4 × 21.9 m / 497 × 71.9 ft; Two geared turbines, General Electric Co; Single screw; 7,400 kW (9,900 SHP); 19 kn; Passengers: 2,500; Crew: 190; Private cars: 165.

1945 Jul: Completed as C4 cargo vessel *Marine Star* for US Maritime Commission. 10,780 GRT.
1952 Sold to Sand Products Corp, Detroit. Converted to passenger carrying by Todd Shipyards Corp, Brooklyn, and West Michigan Dock & Market Corp.
1955 Sep: Commissioned as *Aquarama*.
1956 First crossing on Lake Erie during early part of year. Detroit-Cleveland.
1977 Taken out of service and laid up.

Motorship *Achille Lauro*
Achille Lauro, Naples
PoR: Naples

Ex Willem Ruys

Builders: Koninklijke Maats 'De Schelde' NV, Flushing
Yard no: 214
23,629 GRT; 3,937 DWT; 192.4 × 24.9 m / 631 × 78.4 ft; Eight 8-cyl geared diesels, six from builders, two from Sulzer Bros; Twin screw; 23,900 kW (32,000 BHP); 22 kn; Passengers: 1,097.

1939 Jan: Laid down for NV Rotterdamsche Lloyd, Rotterdam.
1940 Hardly any work done during German occupation of Netherlands. Any progress made was reversed by activities of resistance groups.
1946 Jul 1: Launched as *Willem Ruys*.
1947 Nov 21: Delivered to NV Koninklijke Rotterdamsche Lloyd, Rotterdam. 21,119 GRT. Passengers: 900.
Dec 2: Maiden voyage Rotterdam-Indonesia.
1957 Dec: Passenger service to Indonesia withdrawn.
1958 May: First voyage Rotterdam-New York. Following two voyages to Montreal for Europa-Canada Line, converted by Wilton-Fijenoord NV, Schiedam, for round-the-world service.
1959 Mar 7: 23,114 GRT. Passengers: 275 1st class, 770 tourist class. Rotterdam-Suez-Australia-New Zealand-Panama-Rotterdam.
1964 Jan: Sold to Achille Lauro for delivery in following December.
1965 Jan: To Flotta Lauro, Rome. Renamed *Achille Lauro*. Rebuilt and modernised by Cantieri Navali Riuniti, Palermo.
Aug 29: Work considerably delayed by explosion and fire.
1966 Apr 13: First voyage Genoa-Sydney-Wellington. 23,629 GRT. Passengers: 152 1st class, 1,155 tourist class.
1972 May 19: Badly damaged by fire during overhaul at Genoa. Returned to service five months later.
Dec: Service to Australia withdrawn. Cruising only.
1975 Apr 28: Collided in Dardanelles with livestock transport *Yousset* which immediately sank. One dead.
1982 Jan 23: Detained at Tenerife during voyage from Cape Town to Genoa. Lauro Line in financial difficulties. Required by trustees to cancel entire programme of summer sailings.
1983 Jan 28: Arrived at Genoa. Laid up.
1984 Jul: First of several Mediterranean cruises.
1985 Cruising resumed.
Oct 8: While on cruise between Alexandria and Port Said four heavily-armed Arab terrorists seized control of ship and murdered one American passenger.
Oct 9: Terrorists surrendered. Most of passengers, who at time of seizure were on shore excursion, flown back to Italy.
Terrorists were to have been handed over by Egypt to Palestine Liberation Army but plane carrying them forced to land in Sicily by US fighter aircraft.
Oct 16: *Achille Lauro* returned to Genoa.
Whole affair caused strained diplomatic relations between United States, Egypt, Italy, Yugoslavia and Tunisia, and led to resignation of Italian Government.

1 *The* Aquarama, *laid up since 1977.* (Kludas collection.)
2 *The* Achille Lauro. (Klaus-Peter Kiedel.)

Turbine steamer *Flavian*
Flavian Shipping SA, Panama
PoR: Panama

Ex *Flavia*
Ex *Media*

Builders: John Brown & Co Ltd,
Clydebank
Yard no: 629
12,318 GRT; 165.5 × 21.3 m /
556 × 69.9 ft; Two sets geared
turbines from builders; Twin
screw; 11,200 kW (15,000 SHP);
18 kn; Passengers: 750.

1946 Dec 12: Launched as *Media*
for Cunard-White Star Ltd,
Liverpool.
1947 Aug: Completed. 13,345
GRT. Passengers: 250 in one class;
Crew: 184.
Aug 20: Maiden voyage Liverpool-
New York.
1961 Oct: Sold to Cia Genovese
d'Armamento (Cogedar), Genoa.
Renamed *Flavia*. To 1962 rebuilt
and modernised by Officine
Allestimento & Riparazioni Navi
Ltd, Genoa. 15,465 GRT. Length
overall 169.8 m / 557 ft.
Passengers: 1,224 in one class.
1962 Sep: First voyage Genoa-
Sydney.
Dec: Bremerhaven-Sydney service.
1963 Rotterdam-Panama-New
Zealand-Australia-Mediterranean-
Rotterdam service.
1968 Cruising.
1969 Sold to Costa Armatori SpA,
Genoa. Cruising from Miami.
1982 Sold to Flavian Shipping SA,
Panama. Renamed *Flavian*
Oct 25: Laid up at Hong Kong.

Turbine steamer *Nancowry*
The Shipping Corporation of
India Ltd, Bombay
PoR: Bombay

Ex *Karanja*

Builders: A. Stephen & Sons,
Glasgow
Yard no: 611
10,294 GRT; 8,750 DWT; 157.0 ×
20.1 m / 515 × 65.9 ft; Two sets
geared turbines from builders;
Twin screw; 7,250 kW (9,700
SHP); 16 kn; Passengers: 60 1st
class, 180 2nd class, 800 3rd class.

1948 Mar 10: Launched as
Karanja for British India Steam
Navigation Co Ltd, London.
Oct: Completed.
Bombay-Durban service.
1976 Jun 9: Laid up at Bombay.
Aug: Sold to The Shipping
Corporation of India Ltd,
Bombay. Renamed *Nancowry*.

1 *The laid up* Flavian *in Hong Kong
waters.* (Weirauch collection.)
2 *The* Nancowry *(photographed when
she was the British India liner*
Karanja*) is one of the last passenger
liners.* (Kludas collection.)

1

2

Motorship *Mediterranean Star*
Consolidated Ocean Transports
Ltd, Piraeus
PoR: Piraeus

Ex *Mediterranean Island*
Ex *Patris*
Ex *Bloemfontein Castle*

Builders: Harland & Wolff Ltd,
Belfast
Yard no: 1421
16,259 GRT; 10,922 DWT; 181.2
× 23.2 m / 595 × 76.1 ft; Two 8-
cyl diesels, Burmeister & Wain-
Harland & Wolff; Twin screw;
14,800 kW (20,000 BHP); 18.5 kn;
Passengers: 952; Private cars: 300.

1949 Aug 25: Launched as
Bloemfontein Castle for Union
Castle Mail Steamship Co Ltd,
London.
1950 Mar: Completed. 18,400
GRT. Passengers: 721 cabin class.
Apr 6: Maiden voyage London-
Beira.
1953 Jan 8: Took on board
passengers and crew of Dutch liner
Klipfontein, sinking off
Mozambique.

1959 Nov: Sold to Chandris Bros
and registered at Piraeus as *Patris*
under ownership of National
Greek Australian Line Co Ltd.
Passenger accommodation
reconstructed at North Shields: 36
1st class, 1,000 tourist class.
16,259 GRT.
Dec 14: First voyage Piraeus-
Sydney.
1972 Australia-Singapore service
and cruising from Australian
ports.
1975 Feb 14: Arrived at Darwin
following destruction of port by
tropical storm and remained there
until November, serving as
accommodation ship.
Dec 9: Arrived at Piraeus for
rebuilding as car ferry.
Passengers: 1,000; Private cars:
300.
1976 Jun 17: First voyage Ancona-
Patras service. Then Venice-Patras
service.
1979 Sold to Karageorgis Lines
and registered at Piraeus under
ownership of Consolidated Ocean
Transports. Renamed
Mediterranean Island.

1981 New name *Mediterranean
Star.* Ancona-Patras service.

1

1 *The* Mediterranean Star *sails
between Ancona and Patras.* (Steffen
Weirauch.)
2 *Today the* Independence *cruises
between the Hawaiian islands.*
(Michael D.J. Lennon.)

Turbine steamer *Independence*
American Global Line Inc, New York
PoR: Honolulu

Ex *Oceanic Independence*
Ex *Independence*

Builders: Bethlehem Steel Co, Quincy/Mass
Yard no: 1618
20,220 GRT; 7,250 DWT; 208.0 × 27.1 m / 682 × 88.9 ft; Two sets geared turbines from builders; Twin screw; 41,000 kW (55,000 SHP); 22.5 kn; Passengers: 750.

1950 Jun 3: Launched as *Independence* for American Export Lines Inc, New York.
1951 Jan: Completed. 23,719 GRT. Passengers: 295 1st class, 375 cabin class, 330 tourist class.
Feb 11: Maiden voyage (cruise) New York-Mediterranean.
Apr 12: New York-Genoa, later New York-Naples service.
1959 Feb-Apr: Passenger accommodation reconstructed at Newport News. 110 additional 1st class. 23,754 GRT.

1967 20,251 GRT.
1968 American passenger agency Fugazi operated *Independence* for new style of cruising. Reconstructed as one class ship and exterior given 'pop-art' decoration.
1969 Mar 13: Laid up at Baltimore.
1974 Jan: Sold to Atlantic Far East Lines Inc, Monrovia (C.Y.Tung). Renamed *Oceanic Independence*. Passengers: 950 in one class. Cruising.
1976 Jan 19: Laid up at Hong Kong.
Nov: Reported sold to Shannon SA, Panama, and renamed *Sea Luck 1* but transaction did not proceed.
1979 To Tung group's American Hawaiian Cruise Inc. Repaired and reconstructed by Kawasaki Dockyard Co Ltd, Kobe, and by Ingalls-Taiwan Shipbuilding & Dry Dock Co, Taiwan.
1980 Jun: Seven-day cruises in Hawaiian waters. 20,220 GRT. Passengers: 750.

1981 Sep 24: Ashore off Nawiliwili, Kauai Island, Hawaiian Islands. Passengers taken off and flown home.
Oct 7: To San Francisco for repairs.
1982 Transferred to American Global Line Inc, New York. Renamed *Independence*. Cruising in Hawaiian waters.
1984 Registered in Honolulu.

2

Turbine steamer *Constitution*
American Global Line Inc, New York
PoR: Honolulu

Ex *Oceanic Constitution*
Ex *Constitution*

Builders: Bethlehem Steel Co, Quincy/Mass
Yard no: 1619
20,269 GRT; 7,222 DWT; 208 × 27.2 m / 682 × 89.2 ft; Two sets geared turbines from builders; Twin screw; 41,000 kW (55,000 SHP); 22.5 kn; Passengers: 1,088.

1950 Sep 16: Launched as *Constitution* for American Export Lines Inc, New York.
1951 Jun: Completed. 23,754 GRT. Passengers: 295 1st class, 375 cabin class, 330 tourist class. Jun 25: Maiden voyage New York-Naples-Genoa.
1959 Jan-Mar: Reconstruction at Newport News of 1st class passenger accommodation: 484. 23,754 GRT.
1967 20,269 GRT.
1968 Cruising only.
Sep 9: Laid up at Jacksonville.
1974 Jan: Sold to Atlantic Far East Lines Inc, Monrovia (C.Y. Tung). Renamed *Oceanic Constitution*. Passengers: 950 in one class.
1974 Aug 4: Laid up at Hong Kong.
1981 To Tung group's American Hawaiian Cruise Inc. Overhauled in Taiwan.
1982 Jun: Cruising in Hawaiian waters.
Became *Constitution* of American Global Line, New York.
1984 Registered in Honolulu.

Turbine steamer *Enrico C*
Costa Armatori SpA (Linea 'C'), Genoa
PoR: Naples

Ex *Provence*

Builders: Swan, Hunter & Wigham Richardson Ltd, Newcastle-upon-Tyne
Yard no: 1874
16,495 GRT; 5,802 DWT; 176.5 × 22.3 m / 579 × 73.2 ft; Two sets geared turbines, Parsons Marine Turbine Co; Twin screw; 11,200 kW (15,000 SHP); 18.5 kn; Passengers: 750.

1950 Aug 15: Launched as *Provence* for Société Générale de Transports Maritimes, Marseilles.
1951 Mar: Completed. 15,889 GRT. Passengers: 157 1st class, 167 tourist class, 508 3rd class in cabins, 470 3rd class in dormitories.
Mar 30: Maiden voyage Marseilles-Buenos Aires.
1954 Feb 18: Collided in the River Plate with Liberian tanker *Saxonsea*. *Provence* so badly damaged that not until Jan 1 1955, after temporary repairs at Buenos Aires, was she back at Marseilles where permanent repairs were carried out.
1955 Mar 26: First voyage following above accident, Marseilles-Buenos Aires.
1962 First voyage Genoa-Buenos Aires under charter to Costa Armatori SpA, Genoa.
1965 Sold to Costa Armatori, Genoa. Renamed *Enrico C*. Refitted at Genoa. 13,607 GRT. Passengers: 218 1st class, 980 tourist class.
1966 First voyage Genoa-Buenos Aires.

1972 Cruising only, mainly in the Mediterranean. Passengers: 750.
1980 16,495 GRT.
1984 Naples becomes port of registry.

1 *After many years laid up, in 1982 the* Constitution *returned to service.* (Michael D.J. Lennon.)
2 Enrico C, *the oldest vessel in the Costa fleet.* (Jürgen Saupe.)

Turbine steamer *Amerikanis*
Fifth Transoceanic Shipping Co,
Panama (Chandris Group)
PoR: Panama

Ex *Kenya Castle*

Builders: Harland & Wolff, Ltd,
Belfast
12,795 GRT; 2,866 DWT; 175.7 ×
22.6 m / 576 × 74.1 ft; Two sets
geared turbines, Parsons-Harland
& Wolff; Twin screw; 10,750 kW
(14,400 SHP); 19.5 kn;
Passengers: 911.

1951 Jun 21: Launched as *Kenya
Castle* for Union-Castle Mail
Steamship Co Ltd, London.
1952 Feb: Completed. 17,041
GRT. Passengers: 526 cabin class.
Apr 4: Maiden voyage London-
round Africa.
1967 Apr 22: Laid up in River
Blackwater.
Aug: Sold to Chandris Group and
registered at Piraeus as
Amerikanis under ownership of
National Hellenic American Line
SA.
Converted at Piraeus for North
Atlantic service and cruising.
19,904 GRT.
1968 Aug 8: First voyage Piraeus-
New York, then cruising from
New York.
1970 16,485 GRT. Cruising in
American and European waters.
1980 Transferred to Chandris
America Line SA, Monrovia.
1984 Transferred to Fifth
Transoceanic Shipping Co Ltd,
Panama. 12,795 GRT.

Turbine steamer *United States*
United States Cruises Inc, Seattle/
Wa
PoR: New York

Builders: Newport News
Shipbuilding & Dry Dock Co,
Newport News/Va
Yard no: 488
38,216 GRT; 301.8 × 31.0 m /
990 × 101.7 ft; Four sets geared
turbines, Westinghouse;
Quadruple screw; 130,000 kW
(173,800, max 240,000 SHP); 30,
max 38.32 kn; Passengers: 871 1st
class, 508 cabin class, 549 tourist
class; Crew: 1,093.

1951 Jun 23: Floated out of
building dock for United States
Lines Co, New York.
1952 Jun 21: Delivered.
Jul 3: Maiden voyage New York-
Southampton. *United States* broke
all North Atlantic speed records,
sailing from Ambrose lightship to
Bishop's Rock in three days, ten
hours and 40 minutes at an
average speed of 35.59 knots.
Homeward, she covered the same
stretch in three days, 12 hours and
12 minutes at an average speed of
34.51 knots. This record stands
today.
During winter months route
extended to Bremerhaven.
1961 51,988 GRT.
1962 US measurement 44,893
GRT, reduced to 38,216 GRT in
1967.
1969 Nov 8: Laid up at Newport
News, later at Hampton Roads.
1973 Feb: Bought by US Maritime
Administration. Laid up again, at
Norfolk, Virginia. Offered for sale
several times but always with
stipulation that she should remain
under US flag.

1978 To United States Cruises Inc.
1983 International yards
submitted tenders for
reconstruction of *United States* as
cruise liner. Howaldtswerke-
Deutsche Werft AG, Hamburg,
appeared most promising
contenders.
1984 Sep: Reconstruction contract
signed by owners and
Howaldtswerke-Deutsche Werft.

1 *The* Amerikanis *while cruising.*
(Martin Lochte-Holtgreven.)
2 *The* United States, *still the fastest
passenger ship of all time. The
photograph below shows her off
Bremerhaven.* (Kludas collection.)

Motorship *La Palma*
Intercruise Ltd, Limassol
PoR: Limassol

Ex *La Perla*
Ex *Delphi*
Ex *Ferdinand de Lesseps*

Builders: Forges & Chantiers de la
Gironde, Bordeaux
Yard no: 1
11,608 GRT; 4,128 DWT; 150.1 ×
19.6 m / 492 × 64.3 ft; Two 10-
cyl diesels, Burmeister & Wain-
Chantiers de la Gironde; Twin
screw; 9,100 kW (12,200 BHP); 17
kn; Passengers: 801.

1951 Jul 21: Launched as
Ferdinand de Lesseps for Cie des
Messageries Maritimes, Paris.
1952 Jul: Completed. 10,881
GRT. Passengers: 88 1st class, 112
tourist class, 296 3rd class.
Oct 3: Maiden voyage Marseilles-
Mauritius.
1968 Dec: Sold to C.S.
Efthymiadis, Piraeus.
1969 Renamed *Delphi*. Cruising in
Mediterranean.
1974 Reported sold to Spanish
breakers but transaction did not
proceed.
1976 Nov 11: Laid up at Piraeus.
1977 To Perla Cruises SA,
Limassol, as *La Perla*.
1980 Renamed *La Palma*.
Registered under ownership of
Intercruise Ltd, Limassol.

Motorship *Eros*
Amelia Martin Cia Naviera SA,
Piraeus
PoR: Piraeus

Ex *Chrysovalandou II*
Ex *Patra*
Ex *Olympia*
Ex *Pierre Loti*

Builders: Arsenal de la Marine,
Brest
Yard no: MD4
10,945 GRT; 6,097 DWT; 150.1 ×
19.6 m / 492 × 64.3 ft; Two 10-
cyl diesels, Burmeister & Wain-
Penhoët; Twin screw; 7,700 kW
(10,300 BHP); 17 kn; Passengers:
500.

1952 May 3: Launched as *Pierre
Loti* for Cie des Messageries
Maritimes, Paris.
1953 Jun: Completed. Passengers:
88 1st class, 112 tourist class, 299
3rd class.
Jul 17: Maiden voyage Marseilles-
Mauritius.
1970 Sold to C.S. Efthymiadis,
Piraeus. Renamed *Olympia*.
Mediterranean service.
1972 Renamed *Patra*.
1973/74 Converted to car ferry.
1974 May: First voyage Patras-
Brindisi for Efthymiadis
subsidiary, Hellenic Italian Line
SA.
1978 To Vanieros Ultramar
Armadora SA, Piraeus. Renamed
Chrysovalandou II.
1979 To Amelia Martin Cia Nav as
Eros.

1

Turbine steamer *Carla C*
Costa Armatori SpA, Naples
PoR: Naples

Ex *Flandre*

Builders: Soc des Ateliers &
Chantiers de France, Dunkirk
Yard no: 206
19,942 GRT; 5,280 DWT; 182.8 ×
24.5 m / 600 × 80.4 ft; Two 20-
cyl geared diesels, Stork-
Werkspoor; Twin screw; 19,650
kW (26,700 BHP); 17 kn;
Passengers: 823.

1951 Oct 31: Launched as *Flandre*
for Cie Générale Transatlantique,
Paris.

1952 Jul 8: Delivered. 20,469
GRT. Geared turbines, Rateau
Chantiers de Bretagne; 44,000
SHP; 22 kn; Passengers: 402 1st
class, 285 cabin class, 97 tourist
class; Crew: 361.
Jul 23: Maiden voyage Le Havre-
New York. Withdrawn because of
various mechanical problems and
remained with builders until April
1953.
1953 Apr 17: Returned to Le
Havre-New York service.
1955 Passengers: 212 1st class, 511
tourist class.
1958 *Flandre,* hitherto employed
with sister *Antilles* on Central
America service during winter, on
New York route throughout year.
1962 Following entry into service
of *France, Flandre* used only for
West Indies service and cruising.
White hull.
1968 Feb: Sold to Costa Armatori
SpA, Genoa. Renamed *Carla C.*
Refitting in Italy until December.
19,975 GRT. Passengers: 754.
1969 Jan 10: First cruise Los
Angeles-Mexico. Since 1970,
cruising from US East Coast
ports.
1974 Jun 1: Arrived at Amsterdam
for conversion to motorship.
1975 Jan: Returned to service.
1983 19,942 GRT.

1 *The former* Ferdinand de Lesseps *cruises in the Mediterranean as* La Palma. (Steffen Weirauch.)
2 Eros *is the fifth name for the former* Pierre Loti. (Jürgen Saupe.)
3 *The* Carla C *while chartered to Princess Cruises. A signboard on the boat deck displays her name as* Princess Carla. (A. Bisagno.)

Turbine steamer *Uganda*
P&O Steam Navigation Co,
London
PoR: London

Builders: Barclay, Curle & Co Ltd,
Glasgow
Yard no: 720
16,907 GRT; 5,705 DWT; 164.6 ×
21.7 m / 540 × 71.2 ft; Two sets
geared turbines, Wallsend Slipway
Co; Twin screw; 9,200 kW (12,300
SHP); 17 kn; Passengers: 1,224.

1952 Jan 15: Launched for British
India Steam Navigation Co Ltd,
London.
Jul 17: Completed. 14,430 GRT.
Passengers: 167 1st class, 133
tourist class.
Aug 2: Maiden voyage London-
Beira.
1967 Apr 5: Arrived at Hamburg
for conversion by Howaldtswerke
AG to scholars' cruise ship.
1968 Feb 15: Delivered following
conversion. 16,907 GRT.
Passengers: 1,224.
Feb 27: First cruise.
1973 Registered under ownership
of P&O group, parent company of
British India Steam Navigation Co
Ltd, London.
1982 Falklands war. Requisitioned
by British Government for service
as hospital ship.
Aug 9: Arrived Southampton at
conclusion of service. Partially
refitted for return to cruising.
1983 Jan: Taken over by Ministry
of Defence for two years,
Ascension-Falkland Islands service.
1985 Apr 25: Laid up in River Fal.
1986 May: sold to Taiwan breakers.
On arrival renamed *Triton*.
Aug: Grounded during typhoon.
Turned over on her side. Understood
that breaking up proceeded.

Turbine steamer *Stefan Batory*
Polskie Towarzystwo Okretowe
SA, Gdynia
PoR: Gdynia

Ex *Maasdam*

Builders: Wilton-Fijenoord NV,
Schiedam
Yard no: 733
15,044 GRT; 7,170 DWT; 153.4 ×
21.1 m / 503 × 69.2 ft; Two
geared turbines, General Electric
Co; Single screw; 6,350 kW (8,500
SHP); 16.5 kn; Passengers: 779.

1949 Planned by Holland-
Amerika Lijn as passenger-cargo
vessel *Diemerdijk*.
1952 Apr 5: Launched as
Maasdam.
Jul 15: Completed. 15,024 GRT.
Passengers: 39 1st class, 842
tourist class; Crew: 300.
Aug 11: Maiden voyage
Rotterdam-New York.
1963 Feb 15: On first visit to
Bremerhaven, to which port New
York service was to be extended,
Maasdam struck sunken wrecks of
British cargo vessel *Harborough*
and Soviet cargo vessel
Kholmogory as a result of wreck
buoys having been moved out of
position by drifting ice. Sustained
severe bottom damage and her
master ordered the 500 passengers
to take to the boats. Ship towed to
Norddeutscher Lloyd repair
docks.
Apr 16: First voyage
Bremerhaven-New York.
1966 Rotterdam-Montreal service.
1968 Sold to Polish Ocean Lines,
Gdynia. Renamed *Stefan Batory*.
Refitted at Gdynia.
1969 Apr 11: First voyage Gdynia-
Montreal. Also cruising.

Turbine steamer *Monterey*
International Organisation of
Masters, Mates and Pilots
PoR: San Francisco

Ex *Free State Mariner*

Builders: Bethlehem-Sparrow's
Point Shipyard Inc, Sparrow's
Point, Md
Yard no: 4507
14,799 GRT; 6,558 DWT; 171.8 ×
23.2 m / 564 × 76.1 ft; Two
geared turbines from builders;
Single screw; 14,400 kW (19,250
SHP); 20 kn; Passengers: 365;
Crew: 274.

1952 May 29: Launched as C4
cargo vessel *Free State Mariner* for
US Maritime Commission.
Dec 8: Delivered.
1955 Sold to Matson Navigation
Co, San Francisco.
1956 Rebuilt as passenger ship by
Williamette Iron & Steel Corp,
Portland, Oregon. Renamed
Monterey.
1957 Jan 8: First voyage San
Francisco-Honolulu-Auckland-
Sydney.
1971 Jan: Sold to Pacific Far East
Line Inc, San Francisco. Cruising.
1978 Jan 19: Laid up at San
Francisco.
1979 Apr: Sold to World Airways
Inc. Remained laid up.
1980 Owners understood to be
International Organisation of
Masters, Mates and Pilots. Plans
for recommissioning.

1 *The Falklands War changed life for the* Uganda. *From 1983 to 1985 she operated between Ascension and the Falkland Islands.* (Weirauch collection.)

2 *Replacement of the* Stefan Batory *with a purpose-built vessel has been postponed because of the present situation in Poland.* (Kludas collection.)

3 *The* Monterey *also belongs to the international fleet of laid up passenger ships.* (Martin Lochte-Holtgreven.)

Turbine steamer *Jin Jiang*
China Ocean Shipping Co,
Guangzhou
PoR: Shanghai

Ex *Mariposa*
Ex *Pine Tree Mariner*

Builders: Bethlehem Steel Co,
Quincy/Mass
Yard no: 1624
14,812 GRT; 6,622 DWT; 171.8 ×
23.2 m / 564 × 76.1 ft; Two 16-
cyl diesels, Pielstick-Ishikawajima;
Single screw; 10,592 kW (14,400
BHP); 17 kn; Passengers: 365;
Crew: 274.

1952 Nov 7: Launched as C4 cargo
vessel *Pine Tree Mariner* for US
Maritime Commission.
1953 Apr 3: Delivered. 9,217
GRT. Two geared turbines from
builders; 14,160 kW (19,250
SHP); 20 kn.
1956 Sold to Matson Navigation
Co, San Francisco. Rebuilt as
passenger ship by Williamette Iron
& Steel Corp, Portland, Oregon.
Renamed *Mariposa*.
Oct 27: First voyage San
Francisco-Honolulu-Auckland-
Sydney.
1971 Jan: Sold to Pacific Far East
Line Inc, San Francisco. Cruising.
1978 Apr 7: Laid up at San
Francisco.
1979 Apr: Sold to World Airways
Inc, San Francisco.
1980 Nov 7: In tow of Dutch tug
Zwarte Zee for Mihara, Japan.
Arrived January 6 1981. Laid up.
1981 Returned to Pacific Far East
Line.
1983 Dec: Handed over at Kobe to
China Ocean Shipping Co,
Beijing. Renamed *Jin Jiang*. Re-
engined. Shanghai-Hong Kong
service.

Motorship *Mediterranean Sea*
Mikar Ltd, Piraeus
PoR: Limassol

Ex *City of Exeter*

Builders: Vickers-Armstrongs Ltd,
Newcastle upon Tyne
Yard no: 121
16,384 GRT; 3,283 DWT; 164.9 ×
21.7 m / 541 × 71.2 ft; Two 6-cyl
diesels, Hawthorn-Doxford; Twin
screw; 9,450 kW (12,650 BHP); 16
kn; Passengers: 829.

1952 Jul 7: Launched as *City of
Exeter* for Ellerman Lines Ltd
(Ellerman & Bucknall Steamship
Co Ltd), London.
Apr 29: Delivered. 13,345 GRT.
Passengers: 107 1st class.
May: Maiden voyage London-
Beira.
1971 Sold to M.A. Karageorgis,
Piraeus. Renamed *Mediterranean
Sea*. Rebuilt as car ferry at
Perama. 15,212 GRT. Passengers:
829. Private cars: 400.
1972 Dec: First voyage Patras-
Brindisi-Ancona.
1974 Registered at Famagusta.
16,384 GRT.
1975 Owners recorded as Mikar
Ltd, Limassol, but managed by
Michael A. Karageorgis Lines
Corp.

Motorship *Mediterranean Sky*
Pandiestra Oceanica Navegacion
SA, Piraeus
PoR: Piraeus

Ex *City of York*

Builders: Vickers-Armstrongs Ltd,
Newcastle upon Tyne
Yard no: 122
14,941 GRT; 8,470 DWT; 164.9 ×
21.7 m / 541 × 71.2 ft; Two 6-cyl
diesels, Hawthorn-Doxford; Twin
screw; 9,450 kW (12,650 BHP); 17
kn; Passengers: 786.

1953 Mar 30: Launched as *City of
York* for Ellerman Lines Ltd
(Ellerman & Bucknall Steamship
Co Ltd), London.
Oct 26: Delivered. 13,345 GRT.
Passengers: 107 1st class.
Nov: Maiden voyage London-
Beira.
1971 Sold to M.A. Karageorgis,
Piraeus. Renamed *Mediterranean
Sky*. Rebuilt as car ferry at
Perama. 14,941 GRT. Passengers:
786. Private cars: 400.
1974 Jun: First voyage Ancona-
Rhodes. Registered under
ownership of Pandiestra Oceanica
but managed by Michael A.
Karageorgis Lines Corp.
1984 Laid up.

1 *The* Mariposa *outward bound after
a visit to Hamburg.* (Reinhard
Nerlich.)
2 *As the* Mediterranean Sea, *the one-
time Ellerman liner* City of Exeter *is
no longer recognisable.* (Antonio
Scrimali.)
3 *The* Mediterranean Sky *shows
clearly differences from her sister ship.*
(Antonio Scrimali.)

1

2

3

Turbine steamer *Stella Solaris*
Sun Line Greece Special Shipping
Co Inc, Piraeus
PoR: Piraeus

Ex *Stella V*
Ex *Cambodge*

Builders: Soc des Ateliers &
Chantiers de France, Dunkirk
Yard no: 208
10,595 GRT; 3,400 DWT; 166.2 ×
22.0 m / 545 × 72.2 ft; Two sets
geared turbines, Ateliers &
Chantiers de la Loire; Twin screw;
17,900 kW (24,000 SHP); 21 kn;
Passengers: 660.

1952 Jul 8: Launched as
Cambodge for Cie des Messageries
Maritimes, Marseilles. 13,217
GRT. Passengers: 117 1st class,
110 tourist class, 314 3rd class.
1953 Jul 31: Maiden voyage
Marseilles-Yokohama.
1963 13,520 GRT.
1969 Dec: Sold to Sun Line Greece
Special Shipping Co Inc, Piraeus.
1970 Renamed *Stella V,* then *Stella
Solaris.* Laid up at La Spezia.
1971 Feb: Towed to Piraeus.
Converted at Perama for cruising.
10,595 GRT. Passengers: 660.
1973 Jun 25: First Mediterranean
cruise from Piraeus.
1978 Passengers: 500.
1985 Cruising in Caribbean.

Motorship *Atalante*
Aphrodite Cruises Ltd, Piraeus
PoR: Piraeus

Ex *Tahitien*

Builders: Arsenal de la Marine
National Française, Brest
Yard no: ME 2
12,614 GRT; 8,537 DWT; 167.3 ×
20.6 m / 549 × 67.6 ft; Two 10-
cyl diesels, Soc des Forges &
Ateliers du Creusot; Twin screw;
7,700 kW (10,300 BHP); 17 kn;
Passengers: 659.

1952 Oct 4: Launched as *Tahitien*
for Cie des Messageries Maritimes,
Paris.
1953 Apr: Completed. Passengers:
74 1st class, 84 tourist class, 208
3rd class.
May 4: Maiden voyage Marseilles-
Panama-Sydney.
1972 Sold to Aphrodite Cruises
Ltd, Famagusta. Renamed
Atalante. For cruising in
Mediterranean.
1976 Registered at Limassol. Since
1977, at Piraeus.

1 *As the* Cambodge, *the* Stella Solaris
was a sister ship of the Viet-Nam,
broken up in 1976 as the Malaysia
Kita. *(Peter Voss.)*
2 *Except for the altered cargo
handling gear, house colours and
built-up after section, the* Atlante *is
still recognisable as the former*
Tahitien. *(Kludas collection.)*

Turbine steamer *Leonid Sobinov*
Black Sea Shipping Co, Odessa
PoR: Odessa

Ex *Carmania*
Ex *Saxonia*

Builders: John Brown & Co
(Clydebank) Ltd, Clydebank
Yard no: 692
21,846 GRT; 8,836 DWT; 185.4 ×
24.5 m / 608 × 80.4 ft; Two sets
geared turbines from builders;
Twin screw; 18,300 kW (24,500
SHP); 20 kn; Passengers: 929.

1954 Feb 17: Launched as *Saxonia*
for Cunard Steamship Co Ltd,
Liverpool.
Aug: Completed. 21,637 GRT.
Passengers: 110 1st class, 819
tourist class. Crew: 461.
Sep 2: Maiden voyage Liverpool-
Montreal.
1957 Jun 19: First voyage
Southampton-Montreal.
1961 Apr: First voyage Liverpool-
New York.
1962/63 Refitted at Clydebank by
builders. 22,592 GRT. Renamed
Carmania. Hull and
superstructure painted bright
green. Passengers: 117 1st class,
764 tourist class.
1963 Apr 8: First voyage
Rotterdam-Montreal. Cruising
from US ports in winter.
1967 Painted white. Cruising only.
1969 21,370 GRT.
1971 Oct: Laid up. In December
offered for sale.
1973 Aug: Sold to Nikreis
Maritime Corp, Panama, acting as
agents for Soviet state shipping
company. Renamed *Leonid
Sobinov.*
1974 Feb 25: First voyage
Southampton-Sydney, then
principally cruising in Australian

and Far East waters.
1983 21,846 GRT.

Turbine steamer *Fedor Shalyapin*
Far Eastern Shipping Co,
Vladivostok
PoR: Vladivostok

Ex *Franconia*
Ex *Ivernia*

Builders: John Brown & Co
(Clydebank) Ltd, Clydebank
Yard no: 693
21,406 GRT; 8,472 DWT; 185.4 ×
24.5 m / 608 × 80.4 ft; Two sets
geared turbines from builders;
Twin screw; 18,300 kW (24,500
SHP); 20 kn; Passengers: 800.

1954 Dec 14: Launched as *Ivernia*
for Cunard Steamship Co Ltd,
Liverpool.
1955 Jun: Completed. 21,717
GRT. Passengers: 110 1st class,
833 tourist class; Crew: 461.
Jul 1: Maiden voyage Greenock-
Montreal.
Jul 27: First voyage Liverpool-
Montreal.
1957 Apr 17: First voyage
Southampton-Montreal.
1962 Oct: Refitted by builders
until June 1963. New passenger
accommodation: 119 1st class, 728
tourist class. 22,637 GRT. Painted
green like *Carmania.*
1963 Jan 1: Renamed *Franconia.*
Jul: First voyage Rotterdam-
Montreal.
1967 Painted white.
1969 21,406 GRT.
1970 Cruising only.
1971 Oct: Laid up. In December
offered for sale.
1973 Aug: Sold to Nikreis
Maritime Corp, Panama, acting as

agents for Soviet state shipping
company.
Nov 20: First voyage under new
name, *Fedor Shalyapin,*
Southampton-Sydney-Auckland,
then cruising in Australian and Far
East waters. Cruising also in
European waters.
1985 Lloyd's Register lists the ship
as *Fyodor Shalyapin.*

*1/2 Outwardly almost unchanged,
these former Cunard liners today sail
under the Soviet flag. Above, the*
Leonid Sobinov; *below, the* Fedor
Shalyapin. *(Reinhard Nerlich/Peter
Voss.)*

Turbine steamer *Fairsea*
Sitmar Cruises Inc, Monrovia
PoR: Monrovia

Ex *Fairland*
Ex *Carinthia*

Builders: John Brown & Co
(Clydebank) Ltd, Clydebank
Yard no: 699
16,627 GRT; 9,509 DWT; 185.4 ×
24.5 m / 608 × 80.4 ft; Two sets
geared turbines from builders;
Twin screw; 18,300 kW (24,500
SHP); 20 kn; Passengers: 906.

1955 Dec 14: Launched as
Carinthia for Cunard Steamship
Co Ltd, Liverpool.
1956 Jun: Completed. 21,947
GRT. Passengers: 154 1st class,
714 tourist class. Crew: 461.
Jun 27: Maiden voyage Liverpool-
Montreal. In winter, Liverpool-
New York.
1967 Painted white. Cruising only.
1968 Jan: Sold to Fairland
Shipping Corp, Monrovia.
Renamed *Fairland*. Intended for
Southampton-New Zealand
service of Sitmar Line but laid up
at Southampton.
1970 Feb 21: Arrived at Trieste for
conversion to cruise liner. 21,916
GRT.
1971 Renamed *Fairsea*. Registered
at Monrovia under ownership of
Fairsea Shipping Corp.
1972 Jul: After further
conversion, accommodation for
884 passengers. Cruising from US
ports. 16,627 GRT.

Turbine steamer *Fairwind*
Sitmar Cruises Inc, Monrovia
PoR: Monrovia

Ex *Sylvania*

Builders: John Brown & Co
(Clydebank) Ltd, Clydebank
Yard no: 700
16,667 GRT; 9,495 DWT; 185.4 ×
24.5 m / 608 × 80.4 ft; Two sets
geared turbines from builders;
Twin screw; 18,300 kW (24,500
SHP); 20 kn; Passengers: 906.

1956 Nov 22: Launched as
Sylvania for Cunard Steamship Co
Ltd, Liverpool.
1957 Jun: Completed. 21,989
GRT. Passengers: 154 1st class,
724 tourist class. Crew: 461.
Jun 5: Maiden voyage Greenock-
Montreal.
Jun 26: First voyage Liverpool-
Montreal. In winter Liverpool-
New York.
1965 22,017 GRT.
1967 Painted white. Cruising only.
1968 Sold to Fairwind Shipping
Corp, Monrovia. Renamed
Fairwind. Intended for
Southampton-New Zealand
service of Sitmar Line but laid up
at Southampton.
1970 Jan 14: Arrived at Trieste for
conversion to cruise liner. 21,985
GRT.
1977 16,667 GRT. Cruising from
US ports.

1 *The* Fairsea *dressed overall.*
(Michael D.J. Lennon.)
2 *The* Fairwind. *Launched in 1956 as
the* Sylvania, *she was the last of four
Cunarders to be delivered for the
service to Canada.* (Alberto Bisagno.)

1

2

Motorship *Caribe I*
Olympia Caribbean Shipping Co
Inc, Panama
PoR: Panama

Ex *Caribe*
Ex *Olympia*

Builders: A. Stephen & Sons Ltd,
Glasgow
Yard no: 636
14,533 GRT; 7,860 DWT; 186.1 ×
24.1 m / 611 × 79.1 ft; Two 12-
cyl geared diesels, Klöckner-
Humboldt-Deutz; Twin screw;
10,600 kW (14,100 BHP); 17 kn;
Passengers: 1,200; Crew: 300.

1953 Apr 16: Launched, unnamed,
for Transatlantic Shipping
Corporation, Monrovia (Greek
Line).
Oct 12: Christened *Olympia* and
delivered. 22,979 GRT. Parsons
geared turbines from builders.
25,000 SHP. 21 kn service speed.
Passengers: 138 1st class, 1,169
tourist class.
Oct 15: Maiden voyage Glasgow-
New York, but calling at Belfast,
Liverpool, Dublin and
Southampton as coastwise cruise
for invited guests.
Nov 17: First voyage
Bremerhaven-New York.
1955 Mar 26: First voyage New
York-Piraeus. 17,362 GRT.
1961 Service extended to Haifa.
1968 Registered at Andros under
Greek flag. 17,434 GRT.
1970 Cruising almost exclusively.
Passengers: 1,030 in one class.
1974 Mar 24: Laid up at Piraeus.
1981 Sold to Sally Shipping
GmbH, Bad Schwartau.
Continued laid up at Piraeus but
under German flag. Renamed
Caribe.

1983 Mar 11: Arrived at Hamburg
in tow of *Wotan*. While there,
outward appearance modernised.
Passenger accommodation rebuilt
and machinery installation
renewed. Parsons turbines
exchanged for geared diesels from
Klöckner-Humboldt-Deutz.
Jun 29: On completion of work,
sailed from Hamburg as *Caribe I*.
Caribbean cruising from Miami
for Commodore Cruise Lines.
14,533 GRT.

Turbine steamer *Universe*
Seawise Foundations Inc,
Monrovia
PoR: Monrovia

Ex *Universe Campus*
Ex *Atlantic*
Ex *Badger Mariner*

Builders: Sun Shipbuilding & Dry
Dock Co, Chester/Pa
Yard no: 586
13,950 GRT; 5,182 DWT; 171.8 ×
23.2 m / 564 × 76.1 ft; Two
geared turbines, General Electric
Co; Single screw; 14,350 kW
(19,250 SHP); 20 kn; Passengers:
880.

1953 Jul 1: Launched as C4 cargo
vessel *Badger Mariner* for US
Maritime Commission.
Oct 29: Delivered. 9,214 GRT.
1957 Sold to American Banner
Lines Inc, New York. Rebuilt as
passenger ship by Ingalls
Shipbuilding Corp, Pascagoula.
Renamed *Atlantic*. 14,138 GRT.
Passengers: 40 1st class, 860
tourist class. Crew: 320.
1958 Jun 11: First voyage New
York-Amsterdam.

1959 Oct: Sold to American
Export Lines Inc, New York.
Refitted for Mediterranean service
by Sun Shipbuilding and Dry
Dock Co, Chester.
1960 May 16: First Voyage New
York-Haifa.
1965 Apr: Passengers: 840 in one
class.
1967 Oct 13: Laid up at New
York. From March 1969 at
Baltimore.
1971 Sold to Tung group.
Renamed *Universe Campus*.
Registered under ownership of
Seawise Foundations Inc,
Monrovia. 13,950 GRT.
Sep 4: First cruise from Los
Angeles.
1976 Renamed *Universe*.
1984 Managed by Island
Navigation Corp, Hong Kong.

1 *The* Caribe I, *built as the* Olympia,
*presents herself in modern dress after
ten years laid up.* (Steffen Weirauch.)
2 *In 1976 the* Universe Campus *was
renamed* Universe. (Yoshiaki
Nishimura.)

1

2

Turbine steamer *Azure Seas*
Western Steamship Lines Inc,
Panama
PoR: Panama

Ex *Calypso I*
Ex *Calypso*
Ex *Southern Cross*

Builders: Harland & Wolff Ltd,
Belfast
Yard no: 1498
14,673 GRT; 7,206 DWT; 184.1 ×
23.9 m / 604 × 78.4 ft; Two sets
geared turbines from builders;
Twin screw; 14,900 kW (20,000
SHP); 20 kn; Passengers: 821.

1954 Aug 17: Launched as
Southern Cross for Shaw Savill &
Albion Co Ltd, London.
1955 Feb 23: Delivered. 20,204
GRT. Passengers: 1,160 tourist
class.
Mar 29: Maiden voyage, round-
the-world service from
Southampton.
1968 19,313 GRT.
1971 Cruising from Liverpool.
Nov: Laid up at Southampton.
1972 Apr: Laid up in River Fal.
1973 Jan: Sold to Cia de Vapores
Cerulea SA, Ithaca, on behalf of
Ulysses Line Ltd. Renamed
Calypso.
Mar: Arrived at Piraeus for
conversion to cruise liner. 16,500
GRT. Passengers: 1,000.
1975 Apr 25: First Mediterranean
cruise from Piraeus.
Jun: Cruising from Tilbury or
Southampton for Thomson
Cruises.
1980 Renamed *Calypso I*. Sold to
Eastern Steamship Lines Inc,
Panama. New name *Azure Seas*.
1981 Owners recorded as Western
Steamship Lines Inc, Panama.
14,673 GRT.

Turbine steamer *Carnivale*
Fairweather International Corp,
Panama
PoR: Panama

Ex *Queen Anna Maria*
Ex *Empress of Britain*

Builders: Fairfield Shipbuilding &
Engineering Co Ltd, Glasgow
Yard no: 731
18,952 GRT; 8,912 DWT; 195.1 ×
26.0 m / 640 × 85.3 ft; Two sets
geared turbines from builders;
Twin screw: 22,400 kW (30,000
SHP); 20 kn; Passengers: 1,297.

1955 Jun 22: Launched as *Empress
of Britain* for Canadian Pacific
Steamships Ltd, Liverpool.
1956 Mar 9-10: Trials. 25,516
GRT. Passengers: 160 1st class,
894 tourist class. Crew: 464.
Apr 20: Maiden voyage
Liverpool-Montreal. She had
previously made two short cruises.
1964 Feb: Sold to Greek Line
(Transoceanic Navigation Corp),
Andros.
Nov 16: Handed over.
Nov 18: Renamed *Queen Anna
Maria*.
From November 1964 to March 6
1965 refitted at Mariotti yard,
Genoa. 21,716 GRT. Passengers:
168 1st class, 1,145 tourist class,
741 while cruising.
1965 Mar 24: First voyage Piraeus-
New York. Haifa-New York
service. Cruising.
1975 Jan 22: Laid up at Piraeus.
Dec: Sold to Carnival Cruise Lines
Inc, Miami. Renamed *Carnivale*.
1976 Feb: First cruise in
Caribbean. Registered under
ownership of Fairweather
International Corp, Panama.
18,952 GRT.

1 The Calypso I *shortly before she was
renamed* Azure Seas. *(Weirauch
collection.)*
2 The Carnivale *offers her passengers
plenty of open deck space. (Bill Miller
collection.)*

Turbine steamer *Fairstar*
Fairstar Shipping Corp, Monrovia
PoR: Monrovia

Ex *Oxfordshire*

Builders: Fairfield Shipbuilding &
Engineering Co Ltd, Glasgow
Yard no: 775
21,619 GRT; 7,722 DWT; 185.8 ×
23.8 m / 610 × 78.1 ft; Two sets
geared turbines from builders;
Twin screw; 13,400 kW (18,000
SHP); 20 kn; Passengers: 1,300.

1955 Dec 15: Launched as
Oxfordshire for Bibby Line Ltd,
Liverpool.
1957 Feb 13: Delivered. 20,586
GRT. Passengers: 220 1st class,
100 2nd class, 180 3rd class, 1,000
troops. Crew: 409.
Built as troop transport for service
between Great Britain and
overseas possessions. Ministry of
Transport bore share of cost.
1962 At end of year British
government terminated charter
agreement and ship placed at
disposal of owners.
1963 Chartered for six years to
Fairline Shipping Corp (Sitmar),
Monrovia.
May 20: Arrived at Schiedam for
conversion by Wilton-Fijenoord
NV for Australia service.
1964 Mar: Purchased by Fairstar
Shipping Corp, Monrovia.
Renamed *Fairstar*.
Apr: Conversion completed by
Harland & Wolff Ltd,
Southampton.
May: 21,619 GRT. Passengers:
1,870 in one class.
May 19: First voyage
Southampton-Brisbane.
1973 Aug 20: First cruise from
Sydney. Cruising only.

Motorship *Regent Sea*
Universal Glow Inc, Piraeus
(Regency Cruises)
PoR: Panama

Ex *Samantha*
Ex *Navarino*
Ex *Gripsholm*

Builders: Ansaldo SpA, Genoa
Sestri
Yard no: 1500
17,234 GRT; 3,885 DWT; 192.4 ×
24.9 m / 631 × 81.7 ft; Two 9-cyl
diesels, Götaverken; Twin screw;
12,100 kW (16,200 BHP); 18 kn;
Passengers: 650.

1956 Apr 8: Launched as
Gripsholm for Svenska Amerika
Linien A/B, Gothenburg.
1957 Apr: Completed. 23,191
GRT. Passengers: 150 1st class,
692 tourist class. Crew: 364.
May 14: Maiden voyage
Gothenburg-New York.
1966 23,216 GRT.
1972 22,725 GRT. Mainly
cruising.
1975 Nov: Sold to Michael A.
Karageorgis, Piraeus. Renamed
Navarino. Owners recorded as
Nautilus Armadora SA.
1976 May 22: Following overhaul,
first cruise Venice-Mediterranean.
17,392 GRT. Passengers: 650.
Worldwide cruising.
1981 Aug 8: Aground off Patmos
and badly damaged.
Oct 24: Sold to Sally Shipping
GmbH, Bad Schwartau. Planned
to sail for Commodore Cruises
when repaired.
Oct 29: Bound from Piraeus to
Skaramanga, to be overhauled for
new owner, when fire destroyed
part of passenger accommodation.
Nov 26: Floating dock in which

Navarino lay took 35-degree list.
Ship so badly damaged as to
appear to be total loss.
1982 May 13: Following difficult
salvage operation, Neptun
Transport & Marine Services
(UK), working with Roda A/B,
Gothenburg, and Nicolas E.
Vernicos Shipping Co Ltd,
Piraeus, succeeded in undocking
Navarino. Sally group withdrew
from intention to purchase. To
Greek buyers for use as
accommodation ship.
1983 Jun: Laid up at La Spezia.
Sold to Multiship Italia I Srl,
Rome. Renamed *Navarino*.
1984 Sold to Antonios Lelakis.
Oct 13: Arrived at Piraeus in tow
of *Tore* for repairs at Eleusis yard.
Renamed *Regent Sea*. Operation
of vessel by Regent Sea Cruises on
US market from November 1985.

1 *The* Fairstar *at Southampton shortly
after coming into service.* (Kludas
collection.)
2 *Since 1981 bad luck has dogged the*
Navarino. *Meanwhile she has taken
the name* Regent Sea. (Otto-H.
Nachtigall.)

Turbine steamer *Rhapsody*
Artus Investment Inc, Panama
PoR: Nassau

Ex *Statendam*

Builders: Wilton-Fijenoord NV,
Schiedam
Yard no: 753
24,413 GRT; 6,385 DWT; 195.8 ×
24.7 m / 642 × 81.0 ft; Two sets
geared turbines from builders;
Twin screw; 16,400 kW (22,000
SHP); 19 kn; Passengers: 650.

1956 Jun 12: Floated out of
building dock, unnamed, to order
of Holland-Amerika Lijn,
Rotterdam.
Dec 15: Trials. Had to be towed
back to shipyard because of
machinery damage.
1957 Jan 23: Named *Statendam*
during delivery voyage. 24,294
GRT. Passengers: 84 1st class, 867
tourist class. Crew: 437.
Feb 6: Maiden voyage Rotterdam-
New York.
1966 Cruising almost exclusively.
1973 Owners recorded as NV
Statendam, Curaçao. Cruising
from US ports. 24,214 GRT.
1981 Transferred to Holland
America Cruises Inc, Curaçao.
1982 Oct: Sold to Artus
Investment Inc, Panama.
Renamed *Rhapsody*. Managed by
Paquet Cruises Inc. Continued
cruising from North American
ports.
1984 Mar 28: Grounded near
Georgetown, Grand Cayman.
Mar 31: Passengers taken off.
Jun 15: Refloated. To Galveston
for repairs.
Sep: Re-entered service from Port
Everglades.

1986 Mar: Reported sold to
interests managed by Universal
Glow Ltd, Piraeus. To fly
Panamanian flag. Conversion to
diesel propulsion proposed.

Turbine steamer *Ausonia*
Ausonia Crociere SpA, Naples
PoR: Naples

Builders: Cantieri Riuniti
dell' Adriatico, Monfalcone
Yard no: 1821
12,368 GRT; 3,542 DWT; 159.3 ×
21.1 m / 523 × 69.2 ft; Two sets
geared turbines from builders;
Twin screw; 13,000 kW (17,400
SHP); 20.7 kn; Passengers: 750;
Crew: 215.

1956 Aug 5: Launched for
Adriatica SpA di Navigazione.
1957 Sep 23: Delivered.
Trieste-Beirut service. 11,879
GRT. Passengers: 185 1st class,
135 2nd class, 252 3rd class.
1978/79 Converted for cruising by
Arsenale Triestino SpA, San
Marco. Mediterranean cruises for
Italia Crociere Internazionali SpA,
Genoa. Passengers: 690.
1983 Registered under ownership
of Ausonia Crociere SpA, Naples.
1984 Refitted. 11,921 GRT.
Passengers: 750.
1985 Sep: 12,368 GRT.

1 *The former* Statendam *in her new
dress as the* Rhapsody. (Martin
Lochte-Holtgreven.)
2 *Recent alterations have not added to
the former beauty of the* Ausonia.
(Antonio Scrimali.)

1

2

Motorship *Mermoz*
Chargeurs Savamo (Paquet
Cruises), Marseilles
PoR: Nassau

Ex *Jean Mermoz*

Builders: Chantiers de
l'Atlantique (Penhoët-Loire), St
Nazaire
Yard no: D 17
13,804 GRT; 3,459 DWT; 162.0 ×
19.8 m / 531 × 65.0 ft; Two 7-cyl
diesels, Burmeister & Wain-
Chantiers de l'Atlantique; Twin
screw; 8,000 kW (10,600 BHP); 17
kn; Passengers: 757; Crew: 264.

1956 Nov 17: Launched as *Jean
Mermoz* for Cie de Navigation
Fraissinet & Cyprien Fabre,
Marseilles.
1957 May: Completed. 12,460
GRT. Passengers: 144 1st class,
140 2nd class, 110 3rd class, 460
troops. Crew: 160.
Marseilles-Pointe Noire service.
1965 To Nouvelle Cie de
Paquebots, Marseilles.
1970 Rebuilt as cruise liner by
Mariotti, Genoa. 13,804 GRT.
Renamed *Mermoz*.
Sep: First cruise.
1984 Transferred to Chargeurs
Savamo (Paquet Cruises),
Marseilles.
1985 Jan 9: Returned to service
after a three month refit by
Ateliers & Chantiers de Marseilles
Provence.

Turbine steamer *Shanghai*
Shanghai Haixing Shipping Co,
Shanghai
PoR: Shanghai

Ex *Kengshin*
Ex *Cathay*
Ex *Baudouinville*

Builders: SA Cockerill-Ougrée,
Hoboken
Yard no: 778
13,333 GRT; 10,170 DWT; 170.0
× 21.4 m / 558 × 70.2 ft; Two
geared turbines from builders;
Single screw; 9,300 kW (12,500
SHP); 16.5 kn; Passengers: 300;
Crew: 196.

1957 Jan 10: Launched as
Baudouinville for Cie Maritime
Belge (Lloyd Royal) SA, Antwerp.
Oct 17-19: Trials. 13,922 GRT.
Nov 2: Maiden voyage Antwerp-
Matadi.
1961 Jan: Sold to P&O Steam
Navigation Co, London. Renamed
Cathay. Passengers: 231 in one
class. 13,809 GRT.
Apr 14: First voyage London-
Yokohama.
1969 13,531 GRT.
1970 Recorded as owned by
Eastern & Australian Steam Ship
Co Ltd, London. Far East-
Australia service.
1976 Sold to People's Republic of
China. Renamed *Kengshin,* later
Shanghai.
1979 Service from Chinese ports to
Hong Kong.
1984 Transferred to Shanghai
Haixing Shipping Co, Shanghai.
13,333 GRT.

1

2

1 *The* Mermoz *was also successful in the Caribbean.*

2 *The* Shanghai *in 1978, during a spell in shipyard hands.* (Laurence Dunn.)

Turbine steamer *Royale*
Premier Cruise Line Ltd
PoR: Panama

Ex *Federico C*

Builders: SA Ansaldo, Genoa-
Sestri
Yard no: 1516
15,483 GRT; 5,671 DWT; 184.6 ×
24.0 m / 606 × 78.7 ft; Two sets
geared turbines from builders;
Twin screw; 21,350 kW (28,600
SHP); 21 kn; Passengers: 1,259.

1957 Mar 31: Launched as
Federico C for Lloyd Tirrenico
SpA, Genoa.
1958 Mar: Completed. Passengers:
243 1st class, 300 2nd class, 736
3rd class. 20,146 GRT.
Mar 22: Maiden voyage Genoa-
Buenos Aires. Cruising.
1968 Passengers: 186 1st class,
1,450 tourist class.
1983 Dec: Sold by Costa Armatori
SpA (Linea 'C'), Genoa, to
Premier Cruise Line, Panama, for
cruising from US ports. Renamed
Royale.
1984 Feb: Commenced cruising
from Port Canaveral.
1985 Registered under ownership
of Premier Cruise Line Ltd,
agents: Florida Tec Nauta Inc,
Miami.

Turbine steamer *Santa Rosa*
Vintero Corp, New York
PoR: New York

Builders: Newport News
Shipbuilding & Dry Dock Co,
Newport News/Va
Yard no: 521
11,353 GRT; 8,853 DWT; 177.9 ×
25.6 m / 584 × 84.0 ft; Two sets
geared turbines, General Electric
Co; Twin screw; 16,400 kW
(22,000 SHP); 20 kn; Passengers:
300; Crew: 246.

1957 Aug 28: Launched as *Santa
Rosa* for Grace Line Inc, New
York.
1958 Jun 12: Delivered. 15,371
GRT.
New York-Central America
service.
1959 Mar 26: *Santa Rosa* collided
with US tanker *Valchem,* 22
nautical miles off Atlantic City,
NJ. Both ships badly damaged and
one crewman died aboard the
tanker. Forepart of *Santa Rosa*
burned out.
1967 11,353 GRT.
1970 Grace Line Inc amalgamated
with Prudential Line Inc, New
York, to form Prudential-Grace
Lines Inc. New company adopted
'Prudential' funnel colours.
1971 Jan 22: Laid up at Hampton
Roads.
1975 Handed over to US
Department of Commerce.
Continued laid up.
1976 Sold to Vintero Corp. Laid
up at Baltimore.

1 *The* Federico C *moving away from the Columbus Quay, Bremerhaven, in 1981.* (Peter Voss.)

2 *The* Santa Rosa *has been rusting away at Baltimore since 1976.* (Arnold Kludas.)

Turbine steamer *Liberté*
American Hawaiian Cruises
PoR:

Ex *Island Sun*
Ex *Volendam*
Ex *Monarch Sun*
Ex *Volendam*
Ex *Brasil*

Builders: Ingalls Shipbuilding
Corp, Pascagoula, Miss
Yard no: 467
13,680 GRT; 8,706 DWT; 188.2 ×
26.2 m / 617 × 86.0 ft; Two sets
geared turbines, General Electric
Co; Twin screw; 19,000 kW
(25,500 SHP); 21 kn; Passengers:
679.

1957 Dec 16: Launched as *Brasil*
for Moore-McCormack Lines Inc,
New York.
1958 Sep 5: Delivered. 14,984
GRT. Passengers: 553 1st class.
Crew 401. 35,000 SHP for
maximum 24 knots.
Sep 12: Maiden voyage New York-
Buenos Aires.
1963 Refitted at Baltimore by

Bethlehem Steel Co. 15,257 GRT.
1969 Sep 5: Laid up at Baltimore.
1971 Apr: Sold to Holland
Amerika Lijn.
1972 Aug: Handed over. Renamed
Volendam.
Aug 18: Arrived at Bremerhaven.
Rebuilt at Hapag-Lloyd yard.
Registered under ownership of
Cruiseship NV, Curaçao.
1973 Feb: To Rotterdam for
further alterations.
Apr: Cruise liner. 23,395 GRT.
1974 Jan 6: Laid up at Hampton
Roads.
1975 Aug: Chartered for two years
to Monarch Cruise Lines Inc.
Renamed *Monarch Sun*. Cruising
in Caribbean.
1976 Holland Amerika Lijn
bought Monarch Cruise Lines Inc.
Monarch Sun to sail under
Panama flag. 15,631 GRT.
1977 Transferred to NV
Volendam, Panama. Renamed
Volendam. 15,334 GRT.
1982 Owners recorded as Holland
America Cruises Inc, Curaçao.
23,858 GRT. Cruising from US

ports.
1983 Sold to Banstead Shipping
Ltd, Panama.
1984 Renamed *Island Sun*.
Cruising from US ports. 13,680
GRT.
1985 Sold to American Hawaiian
Cruises. Renamed *Liberté*. To be
used for seven-day cruises to
Tahiti following $25 million
refurbishment. First cruise
planned from Papeete, 21
December.

1 *The* Volendam *passes the Statue of
Liberty, New York*. (Holland-America
Cruises.)

Turbine steamer *Bermuda Star*
Billingshurst Shipping Ltd,
Panama
PoR: Panama

Ex *Veendam*
Ex *Monarch Star*
Ex *Veendam*
Ex *Brasil*
Ex *Veendam*
Ex *Argentina*

Builders: Ingalls Shipbuilding
Corp, Pascagoula/Miss
Yard no: 468
14,208 GRT; 8,706 DWT; 188.2 ×
26.2 m / 617 × 86.0 ft; Two sets
geared turbines, General Electric
Co; Twin screw; 19,000 kW
(25,500 SHP); 21 kn; Passengers:
671.

1958 Mar 12: Launched as
Argentina for Moore-McCormack
Lines Inc, New York.
Dec 9: Delivered. 14,984 GRT.
Passengers: 553 1st class. Crew
401. 35,000 SHP for maximum 24
knots.
Dec 12: Maiden voyage New York-
Buenos Aires.
1963 Refitted at Baltimore by
Bethlehem Steel Co. 15,257 GRT.
1971 Apr: Sold to Holland
Amerika Lijn.
1972 Aug: Handed over. Renamed
Veendam.
Sep 8: Arrived at Bremerhaven.
Rebuilt at Hapag-Lloyd yard.
Registered under ownership of
Cruiseship NV, Curaçao.
1973 Mar: To Rotterdam for
further alterations.
Jun 17: Began service as cruise
liner with voyage from Rotterdam
to New York. 23,372 GRT.
1974 May 14: Laid up at Hampton
Roads.
Dec 15: Chartered to Agência
Maritima 'Intermares' Ltda, Rio
de Janeiro. Renamed *Brasil*.
Cruising from Rio de Janeiro.
1975 Apr: End of charter.
Renamed *Veendam*. Cruising in
Caribbean.
1976 Registered in Panama under
ownership of subsidiary company
Monarch Cruise Lines Inc.
Renamed *Monarch Star*. 15,632
GRT.
1978 Renamed *Veendam*.
Registered in Panama under
ownership of Holland-Amerika
Lijn.
1981 Transferred to Holland
America Cruises Inc, Curaçao.
23,819 GRT. Cruising from US
ports.
1983 Sold to Billingshurst
Shipping Ltd, Panama.
1984 May: Renamed *Bermuda
Star*. Cruising from US ports.
14,208 GRT.

2 *The former* Argentina *has now
carried the name* Veendam *three
times.* (Rudie Kleyn.)

2

Motorship *Hai Xing*
Shanghai Haixing Shipping Co,
Shanghai
PoR: Shanghai

Ex *Yu Hua*
Ex *Nieuw Holland*
Ex *Randfontein*

Builders: Wilton-Fijenoord NV,
Schiedam
Yard no: 760
12,191 GRT; 9,451 DWT; 178.2 ×
21.4 m / 585 × 70.2 ft; Two 6-cyl
diesels, Maschinenfabrik
Augsburg-Nürnberg-Wilton-
Fijenoord; Twin screw; 11,500 kW
(15,400 BHP); 17.5 kn;
Passengers: 297.

1958 Jun 28: Floated out of
building dock for NV Vereenigde
Nederlandsche Scheepv Maats,
The Hague.
Nov 24: Named *Randfontein* and
delivered. 13,694 GRT.
Passengers: 123 1st class, 166
tourist class.
1959 Jan 6: Maiden voyage
Hamburg-Lourenço Marques
service.
1971 Jul: Sold to Koninklijke
Java-China Paketvaart Lijnen
NV.
Aug: Renamed *Nieuw Holland*.
Japan-Australia service. 13,568
GRT.
1974 Sold to People's Republic of
China. Home port Shanghai.
1975 Renamed *Yu Hua*. China-
Africa service. Later China-Hong
Kong.
1981 Renamed *Hai Xing*,
Shanghai Haixing Shipping Co.
1983 12,191 GRT.

Turbine steamer *Rotterdam*
Holland America Cruises Inc,
Curaçao
PoR: Willemstad

Builders: NV Rotterdamsche
Droogdok Maats
Yard no: 300
38,644 GRT; 7,801 DWT; 228.2 ×
28.7 m / 749 × 93.8 ft; Two sets
geared turbines, NV Koninklijke
Maats 'De Schelde'; Twin screw;
28,700 kW (38,500 SHP); 21.5 kn;
Passengers: 1,100.
1958 Sep 13: Launched for
Holland-Amerika Lijn,
Rotterdam.
1959 Jul 12: First trials. 38,645
GRT. Passengers: 655 1st class,
801 tourist class. Crew: 776.
Sep 3: Maiden voyage Rotterdam-
New York.
1968 37,783 GRT.
1969 Cruising only. Passengers:
1,499.
1973 Registered at Willemstad
under ownership of NV
Rotterdam.
1981 Transferred to Holland
America Cruises Inc, Curaçao.
1983 38,644 GRT. Passengers:
1,100.

Turbine steamer *Oriana*
P&O Steam Navigation Co,
London
PoR: London

Builders: Vickers-Armstrongs
(Shipbuilders) Ltd, Barrow-in-
Furness
Yard no: 1061
41,920 GRT; 13,483 DWT; 245.1
× 29.6 m / 804 × 97.1 ft; Two
sets geared turbines from builders;
Twin screw; 59,700 kW (80,000
SHP); 27.5 kn; Passengers: 1,700.

1959 Nov 3: Launched for Orient
Steam Navigation Co Ltd,
London.
1960 May 2: P&O-Orient Lines
(Passenger Services) Ltd formed.
Nov 13: *Oriana* trials. 41,915
GRT. Passengers: 638 1st class,
1,496 tourist class. Crew: 903.
Dec 3: Maiden voyage
Southampton-Sydney, then via
Auckland and US West Coast
ports return to Southampton. Also
cruising.
1965 Outstanding stock of Orient
Steam Navigation Co acquired by
P&O. Owners of *Oriana* recorded
as P&O Steam Navigation Co.
1973 Cruising only.
1986 May: Reported sold to
Japanese Daiwa group.
Transaction arranged by
Mitsubishi group. To be moored
at Beppu Bay, Southern Japan as
a cultural and tourist attraction.
Jun: To be towed to Japan from
Sydney, NSW.

1 *Since 1981 the* Yu Hua *has sailed under the name* Hai Xing. (Jean M. Otten.)
2 *The* Rotterdam *with her blue hull.* (Gerhard Fiebiger.)
3 *The* Oriana *gets up steam.* (Karl-Heinz Schwadtke.)

1

2

3

Turbo-electric ship *Canberra*
P&O Steam Navigation Co,
London
PoR: London

Builders: Harland & Wolff Ltd,
Belfast
Yard no: 1621
44,807 GRT; 8,774 DWT; 249.5 ×
31.1 m / 819 × 102.0 ft; Two
turbines, 65,800 kW (88,200
SHP), driving two generators,
32,200 kW, supplying power to
two electric propulsion motors,
each 42,500 SHP, British
Thomson-Houston Co; Twin
screw: 27.5 kn; Passengers: 1,702.

1960 Mar 1: Launched.
1961 May 18: Trials. Passengers:
538 1st class, 1,650 tourist class.
Crew: 900.
Jun 2: Maiden voyage
Southampton-Sydney-Auckland-
US West Coast-Southampton.
Also cruising.
1962 45,733 GRT.
1963 Jan: Outward bound for
Australia when fire disabled main
engines. Taken in tow by P&O
liner *Stratheden* and with
difficulty brought into Malta as
port of refuge 12 hours later.
Canberra's 1,200 passengers flown
on to Australia.
1968 44,807 GRT.
1973 Cruising only.
1982 Apr 9: Sailed from
Southampton for Falklands as
troopship.
Jul 11: Arrived back at
Southampton following end of
Falklands war.
Sep: Returned to cruising after
reconversion.

Turbine steamer *Mardi Gras*
Carnival Cruise Lines Inc, Miami/
Fl
PoR: Panama

Ex *Empress of Canada*

Builders: Vickers-Armstrongs
(Shipbuilders) Ltd, Newcastle-
upon-Tyne
Yard no: 171
18,261 GRT; 9,551 DWT; 198.1 ×
26.5 m / 650 × 86.9 ft; Two sets
Parsons geared turbines from
builders; Twin screw; 22,400 kW
(30,000 SHP); 20 kn; Passengers:
1,240.

1960 May 10: Launched as
Empress of Canada for Canadian
Pacific Steamships Ltd,
Liverpool.
1961 Mar 7: Trials. 27,284 GRT.
Passengers: 192 1st class, 856
tourist class. Crew: 470.
Apr 24: Maiden voyage Liverpool-
Montreal.
1972 Jan: Sold to Carnival Cruise
Lines Inc, Miami. Renamed *Mardi
Gras*. 18,261 GRT.
Feb 26: First cruise from Tilbury
to Miami. Then cruising from
Miami.

1 *The Falklands War gave the*
Canberra *the popular nickname of
'the Great White Whale'.* (Martin
Lochte-Holtgreven.)
2 *The* Mardi Gras *of Carnival Cruise
Lines is one of the first ships to have
been acquired by that company.*
(Martin Lochte-Holtgreven.)

Turbine steamer *Norway*
Norwegian Caribbean Lines A/S, Oslo
PoR: Oslo

Ex *France*

Builders: Chantiers de l'Atlantique (Penhoët-Loire), St Nazaire
Yard no: G19
70,202 GRT; 13,960 DWT; 315.5 × 33.7 m / 1,035 × 110.6 ft; Two sets geared turbines, Cie Electro-Mécanique-Parsons; Twin screw; 29,850 kW (40,000 SHP); 17 kn; Passengers: 2,400; Crew: 800.

1960 May 11: Launched as *France* for Cie Générale Transatlantique, Paris.
1961 Nov 19: First trials. 66,348 GRT. Passengers: 407 1st class, 1,637 tourist class. Crew: 1,044. Eight sets geared turbines. Quadruple screw. 160,000 SHP. 31, maximum 35 knots.
1962 Jan 19: Cruise, Le Havre-Canary Islands.
Feb 3: Maiden voyage Le Havre-New York route. Also cruising.
1974 Jul: Following French government announcement that no more subsidies were to be paid towards operation of *France,* CGT made it known that they would withdraw their flagship from service with effect from October 25 1974.
Sep: As vessel was about to berth at Le Havre French trade unionists took over from officers and anchored her in fairway. Their action was in protest against threatened loss of jobs. Passengers disembarked by tender.
Oct 9: With situation calmed down, *France* able to berth. Laid up at Le Havre.

1977 Oct: Sold to Saudi Arabian buyer Akkram Ojjeh. Remained laid up at Le Havre.
1979 Jun: Acquired by Lauritz Kloster, Oslo.
Aug: Arrived at Bremerhaven for rebuilding by Hapag-Lloyd as cruise liner. Main machinery reduced to two sets geared turbines developing 40,000 SHP. Twin screw.
Renamed *Norway.*
1980 Apr 14: First trials following conversion. 70,202 GRT.
Jun: First cruise from Miami.
1982 Apr 12: Arrived at Bremerhaven for further alterations by Hapag-Lloyd. Turbo-generators exchanged for diesel-powered installation.
Jul 3: Sailed for Miami upon completion of work.
1984 Sep 2-22: At Blohm + Voss AG, Hamburg, for replacement of steam-driven auxiliary power plant by diesel installation.
Transferred to ownership of Norwegian Caribbean Lines A/S, Oslo.

Turbine steamer *Festivale*
Festivale Maritime Inc, Panama
PoR: Panama

Ex *S. A. Vaal*
Ex *Transvaal Castle*

Builders: John Brown & Co (Clydebank) Ltd, Clydebank
Yard no: 720
26,632 GRT; 16,604 DWT; 231.7 × 27.5 m / 760 × 90.2 ft; Two sets geared turbines from builders; Twin screw; 32,800 kW (44,000 SHP); 23.5 kn; Passengers: 1,432; Crew: 579.

1961 Jan 17: Launched as *Transvaal Castle* for Union-Castle Mail Steamship Co Ltd, London.
Dec 16: Delivered. 32,697 GRT. Passengers: 728 in one class. Crew: 426.
1962 Jan 18: Maiden voyage Southampton-Durban.
1966 Jan 12: Transferred to South African Marine Corp Ltd, Cape Town.
Renamed *S. A. Vaal.* Continued in service under United Kingdom flag.
1967 30,212 GRT.
1969 Feb: Registered in Cape Town.
1977 Apr: Sold to Carnival Cruise Lines Inc. Registered in Panama as *Festivale* under ownership of Festival Maritime Inc (Arison Group), Panama.
Oct 29: Sailed from Southampton for Kobe. Converted there by Kawasaki Heavy Industries Ltd. 164 additional passenger cabins.
1978 Aug 31: Delivered following conversion. 26,632 GRT. Passengers: 1,432. Crew: 579.
Oct 28: First Caribbean cruise.

1 Norway, *the world's largest passenger-carrying vessel.* (Peter Voss.)
2 *The* Festivale. *A photograph taken at Miami during Christmas 1982.* (Martin Lochte-Holtgreven.)

Turbine steamer *Galileo*
Fourth Transoceanic Shipping Co
Ltd, Panama
PoR: Panama

Ex Galileo Galilei

Builders: Cantieri Riuniti
dell'Adriatico, Monfalcone
Yard no: 1862
17,634 GRT; 9,486 DWT; 213.7 ×
28.6 m / 701 × 93.8 ft; Two sets
geared turbines, De Laval-Cantieri
Riuniti dell'Adriatico; Twin
screw; 32,800 kW (44,000 SHP);
25.5 kn; Passengers: 1,700; Crew:
443.

1961 Jul 2: Launched as *Galileo
Galilei* for Lloyd Triestino SpA di
Navigazione, Trieste.
1963 Mar: Completed. 27,888
GRT. Passengers: 156 1st class,
1,594 tourist class.
Apr 22: Maiden voyage Genoa-
Sydney.
1964 27,907 GRT.
1977 Oct 21: Arrived at Palermo
for conversion to cruise liner by
Cantieri Navali Riuniti.
1979 Mar 24: Arrived at Genoa
following conversion. Managed by
Italia Crociere Internazionali SpA,
Genoa. Cruising in
Mediterranean. 28,083 GRT.
Sep 29: Laid up at Genoa.
1980 Sep 6: Laid up again having
made a few cruises.
1981 14-day cruises in
Mediterranean.
Oct 24: Laid up at Genoa.
1983 Nov: Sold to Chandris
Group. Registered under
ownership of Fourth Transoceanic
Shipping Co Ltd, Panama.
1984 Renamed *Galileo*. Refitted
for Caribbean cruising. 18,083
GRT.
1985 17,634 GRT.

Turbine steamer *Costa Riviera*
Costa Armatori SpA (Linea 'C'),
Genoa
PoR: Genoa

Ex Guglielmo Marconi

Builders: Cantieri Riuniti
dell'Adriatico, Monfalcone
Yard no: 1863
28,137 GRT; 9,642 DWT; 213.7 ×
28.6 m / 701 × 93.8 ft; Two sets
geared turbines, De Laval-Cantieri
Riuniti dell'Adriatico; Twin
screw; 32,800 kW (44,000 SHP);
24 kn; Passengers: 1,700; Crew:
443.

1961 Sep 24: Launched as
Guglielmo Marconi for Lloyd
Triestino SpA di Navigazioni,
Trieste.
1963 Oct: Completed. 27,905
GRT. Passengers: 156 1st class,
1,594 tourist class.
Nov 18: Maiden voyage Genoa-
Sydney.
1976 Jan 1: Voyage Naples-River
Plate.
1977 Jun 7: Laid up at Naples.
1978 Jan: Cruising from US ports.
1980 Jan 23: Laid up at Port
Canaveral.
Sep 15: Laid up at Genoa.
1983 Nov: Sold to Costa Armatori
SpA (Linea 'C'), Genoa. Renamed
Costa Riviera. Reconstructed at
Genoa.
1985 Cruising.
Dec: First cruise in Caribbean.

1 *The* Galileo Galilei *at Piraeus while
making one of her few 1981 cruises.*
(Steffen Weirauch.)
2 Costa Riviera *ex* Guglielmo Marconi
after reconstruction. (Antonio
Scrimali.)

1

2

Turbine steamer *Santa Magdalena*
PSS Steamship Co Inc, New York
PoR: San Francisco

Builders: Bethlehem Steel Co,
Sparrow's Point/Md
Yard no: 4585
11,221 GRT; 9,526 DWT; 166.1 ×
24.1 m / 545 × 79.1 ft; Two
geared turbines, General Electric
Co; Single screw; 14,770 kW
(19,800 SHP); 20 kn; Passengers:
121; Crew: 128.

1962 Feb 13: Launched for Grace
Line Inc, New York.
1963 Feb 4: Delivered. 14,443
GRT.
Feb 15: Maiden voyage New York-
Ecuador. Service extended to Peru
following completion of sister
ships.
1967 11,219 GRT.
1970 Grace Line Inc and
Prudential Line Inc amalgamated
to form Prudential-Grace Lines
Inc.
Service from Vancouver, British
Columbia, through Panama
Canal, encircling South America
and returning to Vancouver
having called at 20 intermediate
ports.
1982 Sold to Delta Steamship
Lines Inc, New Orleans.
1984 Nov 30: Withdrawn from
passenger service. Laid up at San
Francisco.
1985 Transferred to PSS
Steamship Co Inc, New York.

Turbine steamer *Santa Mariana*
PSS Steamship Co Inc, New York
PoR: San Francisco

Builders: Bethlehem Steel Co,
Sparrow's Point/Md
Yard no: 4586
11,188 GRT; 9,526 DWT; 166.1 ×
24.1 m / 545 × 79.1 ft; Two
geared turbines, General Electric
Co; Single screw; 14,770 kW
(19,800 SHP); 20 kn; Passengers:
125; Crew: 128.

1962 May 11: Launched for Grace
Line Inc, New York.
1963 Jun 14: Delivered. 14,442
GRT.
New York-Peru service.
1967 11,181 GRT.
1970 Grace Line Inc and
Prudential Line Inc amalgamated
to form Prudential-Grace Lines
Inc.
Service as for *Santa Magdalena*.
1980 Sold to Delta Steamship
Lines Inc, New Orleans.
1982 Dec 21: Laid up at San
Francisco.
1984 Delta Steamship Lines
withdrew from passenger ship
operation.
1985 Transferred to PSS
Steamship Co Inc, New York.

1 *Delta Lines offered a regular service
from US ports rounding South
America. The photograph shows the*
Santa Magdalena. *(Rudie Kleyn.)*
2 *The combined passenger liner and
containership* Santa Mariana. *(Rudie
Kleyn.)*

1

2

Turbine steamer *Santa Maria*
Prudential Lines Inc, New York
PoR: San Francisco

Builders: Bethlehem Steel Co,
Sparrow's Point/Md
Yard no: 4587
11,221 GRT; 9,382 DWT; 166.1 ×
24.1 m / 545 × 79.1 ft; Two
geared turbines, General Electric
Co; Single screw; 14,770 kW
(19,800 SHP); 20 kn; Passengers:
121; Crew: 128.

1962 Oct 9: Launched for Grace
Line Inc, New York.
1963 Sep 23: Delivered. 14,442
GRT.
New York-Peru service.
1967 11,888 GRT.
1970 Grace Line Inc and
Prudential Line Inc amalgamated
to form Prudential-Grace Lines
Inc.
Service as for *Santa Magdalena*.
1982 Sold to Delta Steamship
Lines Inc, New Orleans.
1984 Oct 9: Laid up at San
Francisco following withdrawal by
Delta Steamship Lines of
passenger services.
1985 Transferred to Prudential
Lines Inc, New York.

Motorship *Ming Hua*
Guangzhou Ocean Shipping Co,
Guangzhou
PoR: Guangzhou/Canton

Ex *Ancerville*

Builders: Chantiers de
l'Atlantique (Penhoët-Loire), St
Nazaire
Yard no: M21
14,324 GRT; 3,037 DWT; 168.2 ×
21.8 m / 551 × 71.5 ft; Two 12-
cyl diesels, Burmeister & Wain-
Chantiers de l'Atlantique; Twin
screw; 17,900 kW (24,000 BHP);
20 kn; Passengers: 380.

1962 Apr 5: Launched as
Ancerville for Cie de Navigation
Paquet, Marseilles.
Aug 20: Delivered. Passengers:
171 1st class, 346 tourist class, 253
3rd class. Crew: 173.
Sep 5: Cruise to Canary Islands,
then maiden voyage Marseilles-
Dakar.
1970 Owners Nouvelle Cie de
Paquebots, Marseilles.
1973 Apr: Sold to People's
Republic of China. Renamed
Ming Hua. Service between China
and East Africa.
1981 Cruising from Australia
under control of Burns, Philp &
Co Ltd.
1986 Apr: Understood to be
serving as an accommodation
ship.

1 *The* Santa Maria *off Rio de Janeiro.*
(Delta Lines.)
2 *With the* Ming Hua, *China Ocean
Shipping broke into the international
cruising market.* (Jean M. Otten.)

1

2

Motorship *Ziluolan*
Government of the People's
Republic of China, Guangzhou
PoR: Guangzhou/Canton

Ex *Sakura*
Ex *Sakura Maru*

Builders: Mitsubishi Heavy
Industries, Reorganised, Ltd,
Kobe
Yard no: 933
12,470 GRT; 10,618 DWT; 157.0
× 21.0 m / 515 × 68.9 ft; One 7-
cyl diesel from builders; Single
screw; 7,300 kW (9,800 BHP); 17
kn; Passengers: 948.

1962 Jun 22: Launched as *Sakura
Maru* for Nihon Sangyo Junko
Mihonichi, Kyokai, Tokyo.
Oct 15: Delivered. 12,628 GRT.
Passengers: 152 1st class, 800
tourist class.
Nov 5: Maiden voyage Kobe-
Jeddah. Served as exhibition ship
for Japanese industrial products.
When not so engaged, sailed in
Yokohama-South America
passenger service under
management of Mitsui-OSK Lines
Ltd, Tokyo.
1970 12,470 GRT.
1971 Sold to Mitsubishi Shintaku
Ginko KK, Tokyo. Registered as
Sakura under ownership of
Oshima Unyu KK, Kagoshima.
1973 Jun: Cruising from Tokyo.
1982 Sold to Government of the
People's Republic of China,
Guangzhou. Renamed *Ziluolan*.

Turbine steamer *Royal Odyssey*
Lido Maritime Inc, Piraeus
PoR: Piraeus

Ex *Doric*
Ex *Hanseatic*
Ex *Shalom*

Builders: Chantiers de
l'Atlantique (Penhoët-Loire), St
Nazaire
Yard no: Z21
17,884 GRT; 7,394 DWT; 191.4 ×
24.8 m / 628 × 81.4 ft; Two sets
geared turbines, Parsons-
Chantiers de l'Atlantique; Twin
screw; 18,650 kW (25,000 SHP);
20 kn; Passengers: 817; Crew: 360.

1962 Nov 10: Launched as *Shalom*
for Zim Israel Navigation Co Ltd,
Haifa. Names *King Salomon* and
King David originally considered.
1964 Mar 3: Completed. 25,338
GRT. Passengers: 72 1st class,
1,018 tourist class. Crew: 469.
Apr 17: Maiden voyage Haifa-
New York.
Oct: Passenger accommodation
remodelled by Wilton Fijenoord
NV: 148 1st class, 864 tourist
class.
Nov 26: Collided off New York
with Norwegian tanker *Stolt
Dagali* which broke in two and
sank.
1967 May: Sold to Hanseatic
Schiffahrts GmbH (Deutsch
Atlantik Schiffahrts GmbH),
Hamburg.
Nov 9: Handed over. Renamed
Hanseatic.
Dec 16: First voyage under
German flag, cruise with invited
guests. 25,320 GRT. Hamburg-
New York service and cruising.
1969 Cruising only.
1973 Jul: Sold to Home Lines Inc,
Panama.

Sep 25: Delivered at Genoa.
Renamed *Doric*. Cruising. 17,884
GRT.
1981 Sold to Lido Maritime Inc.
Renamed *Royal Odyssey*.
1982 Jan: Reconstructed at
Perama and Neorion.
May 28: Upon completion of
work, employed on world-wide
cruising. Managed by Royal
Cruise Line.
1984 Jul 10: Collided with Soviet
freighter *Vasya Alekseev* which
sank but was subsequently raised
and refloated. *Royal Odyssey*'s
passengers disembarked at
Copenhagen. Minor damage
repaired at Hamburg.

1 The Sakura *berthed at Yokohama.*
(Yoshiaki Nishimura.)
2 The Royal Odyssey's *new funnel
considerably alters the appearance of
the former* Shalom. *(Martin Lochte-
Holtgreven.)*

Motorship *Ivan Franko*
Black Sea Shipping Co, Odessa
PoR: Odessa

Builders: Mathias-Thesen-Werft, Wismar
Yard no: 125
20,064 GRT; 6,007 DWT; 176.1 × 23.6 m / 578 × 77.4 ft; Two 7-cyl diesels, Sulzer Bros-NV Werkspoor; Twin screw; 15,700 kW (21,000 BHP); 20.5 kn; Passengers: 750; Crew: 220.

1963 Jun 15: Launched.
1964 Nov 14: Delivered. 19,861 GRT.
Cruising and voyages on various routes, for instance Black Sea-Mediterranean and Sydney-Southampton.
1975 Cruising only.

Motorship *Aleksandr Pushkin*
Far East Shipping Co, Leningrad
PoR: Leningrad

Builders: Mathias-Thesen-Werft, Wismar
Yard no: 126
20,502 GRT; 5,180 DWT; 176.3 × 23.6 m / 578 × 77.4 ft; Two 7-cyl diesels, Sulzer Bros-H. Cegielski; Twin screw; 15,700 kW (21,000 BHP); 20.5 kn; Passengers: 750; Crew: 220.

1964 Mar 26: Launched for Baltic Shipping Co, Leningrad.
1965 Jun: Completed. 19,860 GRT. Cruising.
1966 Apr 13: First voyage Leningrad-Montreal. Passengers for North Atlantic voyages: 130 1st class, 620 tourist class.
1975 20,502 GRT. Mainly cruising.
1985 To Far East Shipping Co.

Turbine steamer *Oceanic*
Home Lines Inc, Panama (Soc de Gestion Evge SA, Piraeus)
PoR: Panama

Builders: Cantieri Riuniti dell'Adriatico, Monfalcone
Yard no: 1876
27,645 GRT; 8,738 DWT; 238.4 × 29.4 m / 782 × 96.4 ft; Two sets geared turbines, De Laval-Cantieri Riuniti dell'Adriatico; Twin screw; 45,100 kW (60,500 SHP); 26.5 kn; Passengers: 1,340; Crew: 560.

1963 Jan 15: Launched.
1965 Mar 31: Maiden voyage Genoa-New York. Registered under ownership of Home Lines Inc, Panama.
Apr 24: First cruise New York-Bahamas. Intended originally for Cuxhaven-New York service, *Oceanic* has been used almost exclusively for cruising, making only occasional Atlantic crossings.
1985 Registered under ownership of Soc de Gestion Evge SA, Piraeus.

1

1 *The* Ivan Franko, *name-ship of the class.* (Peter Voss.)
2 *The* Aleksandr Pushkin *in Geiranger Fjord.* Peter Voss.)
3 *The* Oceanic, *flagship of Home Lines for 20 years.* (Michael D.J. Lennon.)

Motorship *Taras Shevchenko*
Black Sea Shipping Co, Odessa
PoR: Odessa

Builders: Mathias-Thesen-Werft,
Wismar
Yard no: 127
20,027 GRT; 6,000 DWT; 176.1 ×
23.6 m / 578 × 77.4 ft; Two 7-cyl
diesels, Sulzer Bros-H. Cegielski;
Twin screw; 15,700 kW (21,000
BHP); 20.5 kn; Passengers: 650;
Crew: 220.

1965 Jan 16: Launched.
1967 Apr 26: Delivered. 19,549
GRT. Passengers: 750.
Cruising.
1974 20,027 GRT. Passengers:
650.

Motorship *Shota Rustaveli*
Black Sea Shipping Co, Odessa
PoR: Odessa

Builders: Mathias-Thesen-Werft,
Wismar
Yard no: 128
20,499 GRT; 5,696 DWT; 175.8 ×
23.6 m / 577 × 77.4 ft; Two 7-cyl
diesels, Sulzer Bros-H. Cegielski;
Twin screw; 15,700 kW (21,000
BHP); 20.5 kn; Passengers: 650;
Crew: 220.

1967 Launched.
1968 Jun 30: Delivered. 19,567
GRT. Passengers: 750. Cruising.
1975 20,146 GRT. Passengers:
650.
1980 20,499 GRT.

Motorship *Mikhail Lermontov*
Baltic Shipping Co, Leningrad
PoR: Leningrad

Builders: Mathias-Thesen-Werft,
Wismar
Yard no: 129
20,352 GRT; 4,956 DWT; 175.8 ×
23.6 m / 577 × 77.4 ft; Two 7-cyl
diesels, Sulzer Bros-H. Cegielski;

Twin screw; 15,700 kW (21,000
BHP); 20.5 kn; Passengers: 700;
Crew: 300.

1970 Dec 31: Launched.
1972 Mar 18: Completed. 19,872
GRT.
Apr 21: Maiden voyage
Bremerhaven-Canary Islands.
Jun 9: First voyage Bremerhaven-
Montreal.
1973 May 28: First voyage
Leningrad-New York. During
summer months, June to August,
North Atlantic service. Otherwise
cruising.
1980 Cruising only.
1982 Jan 6: Arrived at Hapag-
Lloyd yard, Bremerhaven, for
improvements to or renewal of
passenger accommodation. Hull
painted white.
May 21: Work completed.
1986 Feb 16: On cruise from
Sydney, NSW, struck rocks off
South Island, New Zealand, and
sank near Port Gore. One crew
member missing.

1 *The* Taras Shevshenko *in Valetta
Harbour, Malta.* (Peter Voss.)
2 *Since 1983 the* Shota Rustaveli *has
had her hull painted white.* (Peter
Voss.)
3 *The* Mikhail Lermontov *after her
thorough overhaul at Bremerhaven.*
(Peter Voss.)

1

2

3

Motorship *Sagafjord*
Cunard Line Ltd (The Cunard
Steam Ship Co plc, London)
PoR: Nassau

Builders: Forges & Chantiers de
La Méditerranée, La Seyne
Yard no: 1366
24,109 GRT; 6,353 DWT; 188.9 ×
24.5 m / 620 × 80.4 ft; Two 9-cyl
diesels, Sulzer Bros-Forges &
Chantiers de La Méditerranée;
Twin screw; 20,150 kW (27,000
BHP); 20 kn; Passengers: 509;
Crew: 350.

1964 Jun 13: Launched for Den
Norske Amerikalinje A/S, Oslo.
1965 May: First trials.
Sep 18: Delivered. 24,002 GRT.
Passengers: 85 1st class, 704
tourist class.
Oct 2: Maiden voyage Oslo-New
York. Mainly cruising.
Passengers: 462 in one class.
1972 Passengers: 509 in one class.
1980 May: K/S Norwegian
American Cruises A/S, Oslo,
formed to manage *Sagafjord* and
Vistafjord. Ten per cent share held
by Leif Hoegh & Co A/S, Oslo.
Oct: Under reconstruction at
Hamburg by Blohm + Voss AG
until December. Additional deck.
Passengers: 509. 24,109 GRT.
Dec: Leif Hoegh & Co A/S
acquired remaining 90 per cent
share in K/S Norwegian American
Cruises A/S.
1983 May: Sold to Cunard group
for delivery in October, with right
to retain name *Sagafjord* and
goodwill of Norwegian American
Cruises. Later in year funnel
painted in Cunard house colours.
Registered under Bahamian flag.

Motorship *Vistafjord*
Cunard Line Ltd (The Cunard
Steam-Ship Co plc, London)
PoR: Nassau

Builders: Swan Hunter
Shipbuilders Ltd, Wallsend
Yard no: 39
24,492 GRT; 5,954 DWT; 191.1 ×
25.0 m / 627 × 82.0 ft; Two 9-cyl
diesels, Sulzer Bros-G. Clark &
NEM; Twin screw; 17,900 kW
(24,000 BHP); 20 kn; Passengers:
670; Crew: 390.

1972 May 15: Launched for Den
Norske Amerikalinje A/S, Oslo.
1973 Apr 6: Trials.
May 15: Delivered. 24,292 GRT.
May 22: Maiden voyage Oslo-New
York. World-wide cruising.
1980 May: K/S Norwegian
American Cruises A/S, Oslo,
formed to manage *Sagafjord* and
Vistafjord. Ten per cent share held
by Leif Hoegh & Co A/S, Oslo.
Dec: Leif Hoegh & Co A/S
acquired remaining 90 per cent
share in K/S Norwegian American
Cruises A/S.
1983 May: Sold with *Sagafjord* to
Cunard group for delivery in
October, with right to retain name
Vistafjord and goodwill of
Norwegian American Cruises.
Later in year funnel painted in
Cunard house colours. Registered
under Bahamian flag. 24,492
GRT.

1 *With the sale of the* Sagafjord
(illustrated above right) and Vistafjor
*to Cunard, yet another distinguished
chapter in the history of passenger
shipping came to an end.* (Weirauch
collection.)
2 *The* Vistafjord *in 1979, during her
first visit to Bremerhaven.* (Peter
Voss.)

1

2

Turbine steamer *Eugenio C*
Costa Armatori SpA (Linea 'C'),
Genoa
PoR: Naples

Builders: Cantieri Riuniti
dell'Adriatico, Monfalcone
Yard no: 1884
30,567 GRT; 7,810 DWT; 217.5 ×
29.3 m / 714 × 96.1 ft; Two sets
geared turbines, De Laval-Cantieri
Riuniti dell'Adriatico; Twin
screw; 41,000 kW (55,000 SHP);
27 kn; Passengers: 1,603; Crew:
424.

1964 Nov 21: Launched.
1966 Aug 22: Delivered.
Passengers: 178 1st class, 356 2nd
class, 1,102 tourist class.
Genoa-Buenos Aires service.
Cruising.

Motorship *Sea Princess*
Investors in Industry plc
(P&O Passenger Division),
London
PoR: London

Ex *Kungsholm*

Builders: John Brown & Co
(Clydebank) Ltd, Clydebank
Yard no: 728
27,670 GRT; 5,182 DWT; 201.2 ×
26.3 m / 660 × 86.3 ft; Two 9-cyl
diesels, Götaverken; Twin screw;
18,800 kW (25,200 BHP); 21 kn;
Passengers: 720.

1965 Apr 14: Launched as
Kungsholm for Svenska Amerika
Linien A/B, Gothenburg.
Nov 19: First trials.
1966 Mar 17: Delivered. 26,678
GRT. Passengers: 108 1st class,
605 tourist class; 450 in one class
while cruising. Crew: 438.
Apr 22: Maiden voyage
Gothenburg-New York.
Mainly cruising.
1975 Aug: Sold to Flagship
Cruises Ltd, New York.
Oct 6: Handed over. Cruising
from New York. 18,174 GRT.
1978 Sold to P&O Passenger
Division. Registered under
ownership of Finance for Shipping
Ltd, London.
Sep 4: Arrived at Vegesack for
alterations by Bremer Vulkan,
Schiffbau & Maschinenfabrik.
Passengers: 750.
1979 Jan 15: Renamed *Sea
Princess*.
Feb 16: First cruise, Hong Kong to
Sydney. Cruising in Far East and
in Australian waters.
1982 Additional passenger cabins
built in by Vosper Ltd at
Southampton. Passengers: 840.
Cruising in European waters.

1984 Registered under ownership
of Investors in Industry plc.
Passengers: 720.

1 *The* Eugenio C, *flagship of Costa.*
(Arnold Kludas.)
2 *The* Sea Princess *arriving at
Bremerhaven for overhaul.* (Peter
Voss.)

1

2

Motorship *Ocean Princess*
Oceanic Endeavour SA, Panama
PoR: Panama

Ex Italia

Builders: Cantiere Navale
Felszegi, Trieste
Yard no: 76
12,218 GRT; 2,660 DWT; 149.0 ×
20.7 m / 489 × 67.9 ft; Two 9-cyl
diesels, Cantieri Riuniti
dell'Adriatico; Twin screw; 11,050
kW (14,800 BHP); 19 kn;
Passengers: 550.

1965 Apr 28: Launched as *Italia*
for Sunsarda SpA, Trieste.
1967 Aug: Delivered. 12,219 GRT.
Passengers: 452.
Cruising.
In same year sold to Crociere
d'Oltremare SpA, Cagliari.
Service Acapulco-Seattle and
cruising in North American
waters.
1974 Oct: Sold to Costa Armatori
SpA, Cagliari.
1980 12,183 GRT.
1983 Sold to Ocean Cruise Lines,
Athens. Renamed *Ocean Princess*.
Sep 24: Arrived at Piraeus where
refitted. Passengers: 550.
1984 May: First Mediterranean
cruise. Also operation on US
market. 8,469 GRT. Transferred
to Oceanic Endeavour SA,
Panama. 12,218 GRT.

Diesel-electric ship *Ambrose Shea*
CN Marine Inc, Halifax, NS
PoR: St John's

Builders: Marine Industries Ltd,
Sorel, PQ
Yard no: 324
10,093 GRT; 1,691 DWT; 120.6 ×
21.7 m / 396 × 71.2 ft; Five 16-cyl
diesels, 18,050 kW (24,200 BHP),
five generators and two driving
motors, 9,700 kW (13,000 BHP),
Cooper-Bessemer of Canada;
Twin screw; 16.5 kn; Passengers:
258, plus 267 unberthed; Private
cars: 150; Commercial vehicles:
19.

1966 Apr 16: Launched for
Department of Transport,
Government of Canada, Ottawa.
Dec 12: Badly damaged as result
of fire at fitting-out berth.
Delivery delayed.
1967 Dec: Completed.
East coast of Canada service.
1979 Transferred to Canadian
National Marine Inc, Halifax, NS.

1 *The lines of the* Ocean Princess,
illustrated here when she was the
Italia, *cannot be confused with those
of any other ship.* (Steffan Weirauch.)
2 *Contrary to Lloyd's Register,
wherein the gross tonnage of the*
Ambrose Shea *is recorded as 9,934,
she is measured in Canada at 10,093*
(CN Marine.)

1

2

Motorship *Yaohua*
Guangzhou Ocean Shipping Co,
Guangzhou
PoR: Guangzhou/Canton

Builders: Chantiers de
l'Atlantique (Penhoët-Loire), St
Nazaire
Yard no: N23
10,151 GRT; 3,302 DWT; 149.0 ×
21.0 m / 489 × 68.9 ft; Two 9-cyl
diesels, Cie de Construction
Mécanique, Procédés Sulzer; Twin
screw; 11,200 kW (15,000 BHP);
21 kn; Passengers: 100 1st class,
100 2nd class, 118 3rd class; Crew:
177.

1966 Dec 10: Launched.
1967 Aug 20: Delivered to China
Ocean Shipping Co, Beijing.
China-East Africa service, later
employed on routes to Far East.
1983 Cruising on River Yangtse
and along China coast.
1984 Transferred to Guangzhou
Ocean Shipping Co, Guangzhou.

Turbine steamer *Queen
Elizabeth 2*
Cunard Line Ltd, London
PoR: Southampton

Builders: Upper Clyde
Shipbuilders Ltd, Clydebank
Division, Clydebank
Yard no: 736
67,139 GRT; 15,521 DWT; 293.5
× 32.0 m / 963 × 105.0 ft; Two
sets geared turbines, John Brown
Engineering (Clydebank); Twin
screw; 82,100 kW (110,000 SHP);
28.5 kn; Passengers: 647 1st class,
1,223 tourist class, 1,740 in one
class while cruising.

1967 Sep 20: Launched.
1968 Nov 26-29: First trials.
65,863 GRT. Passengers: 564 1st
class, 1,441 tourist class, 1,400 in
one class while cruising. Crew:
906.
Dec 17-19: Second trials.
Dec 23: Maiden cruise Greenock-
Canary Islands, during which
turbine damage forced return to
builders. With passenger
accommodation uncompleted
Cunard refused to accept ship on
planned date, January 1 1969.
1969 Apr 1-8: Renewed trials.
Apr 18: Delivered.
May 2: Maiden voyage
Southampton-New York. Mainly
cruising.
1971 Jan 9: *Queen Elizabeth 2*
took part in rescue of passengers
and crew from French liner
Antilles, on fire in Caribbean.
1972 Passenger accommodation
altered: 604 1st class, 1,223 tourist
class, 1,740 in one class while
cruising. 66,851 GRT.
1974 Apr 1: 270 nautical miles
south-west of Bermudas damaged
fuel pipe put all boilers out of

action, leaving ship without
power. After temporary repair
effected with materials on board
had held for only half an hour,
1,654 passengers were transferred
at sea to Norwegian cruise ship
Sea Venture on April 3.
Apr 5: *Queen Elizabeth 2* taken in
tow by tugs *Joan Moran* and
Elizabeth Moran. On April 7
brought into Hamilton where
damage repaired.
1978 Further extension of
passenger accommodation. 67,140
GRT.
1982 May 12: Requisitioned as
troopship for Falklands war.
Aug 14: Returned to civilian
service following refit. For first
time given traditional Cunard
funnel colours.
1984 67,139 GRT.
1986 Oct: To be converted by
Lloyd Werft AG, Bremerhaven, to
diesel propulsion.

1 *The* Yaohua *is the largest passenger ship to have been purpose-built for the People's Republic of China.* (Chantiers de l'Atlantique.)

2 *During the refit which followed her service in the Falklands War the* Queen Elizabeth 2 *had her hull painted grey as shown in this photograph. However, in the early summer of 1983 it was restored to its former blue-black colour.* (Yoshitatsu Fukawa.)

Turbine steamer *Maksim Gorkiy*
Black Sea Shipping Co, Odessa
PoR: Odessa

Ex *Hanseatic*
Ex *Hamburg*

Builders: Howaldtswerke-
Deutsche Werft AG, Hamburg
Yard no: 825
24,981 GRT; 5,766 DWT; 194.7 ×
26.6 m / 639 × 87.3 ft; Two sets
geared turbines, Allgemeine
Electricitäts Gesellschaft; Twin
screw; 16,900 kW (22,660 SHP);
22 kn; Passengers: 600.

1968 Feb 21: Launched as
Hamburg for Deutsche Atlantik
Linie, Hamburg.
1969 Feb 12-15: Trials. 25,022
GRT. Passengers: 652 in one class.
Crew: 403.
Mar 20: Delivered.
Mar 28: Maiden voyage cruise
Cuxhaven-South America.
1973 24,981 GRT.
Sep 25: Renamed *Hanseatic*.
Dec 1: Deutsche Atlantik Linie in
financial difficulty and suspended
operations. *Hanseatic* laid up at
Hamburg.
Dec 12: Intended sale to Japanese
Ryutsu Kaiun KK having failed to
materialise, ship sold to Robin
International Corp, New York,
acting on behalf of Soviet state
shipping company.
1974 Jan 25: Delivered to Black
Sea Shipping Co, Odessa.
Renamed *Maksim Gorkiy*.
Worldwide cruising.

Diesel-electric ship *John Hamilton Gray*
CN Marine Inc, Halifax/NS
PoR: Charlottetown

Builders: Marine Industries Ltd,
Sorel, PQ
Yard no: 349
11,260 GRT; 3,087 DWT; 122.1 ×
21.1 m / 400 × 69.2 ft; Eight 12-
cyl diesels, 12,000 kW (16,000
BHP), driving eight generators,
each 1,365 kW, supplying power
to electric propulsion motors, two
aft each 6,800 SHP and two
forward each 5,100 SHP,
Fairbanks, Morse (Canada); Twin
screw; 18 kn; Passengers: 1,000
total, cabin accommodation for
ten.

1967 Nov 18: Launched.
1968 Oct: Completed. Car ferry
and ice-breaker, east coast of
Canada.

Motorship *Starward*
K/S A/S Starward, Oslo
PoR: Oslo

Builders: AG 'Weser', Werk
Seebeck, Bremerhaven
Yard no: 935
12,959 GRT; 3,241 DWT; 160.1 ×
22.8 m / 525 × 74.8 ft; Two 16-
cyl diesels, Maschinenfabrik
Augsburg-Nürnberg; Twin screw;
12,950 kW (17,380 BHP); 21 kn;
Passengers: 928; Crew: 225.

1968 Apr 27: 90 m (295 ft) long
after section launched.
Jun 21: Hull floated out of
building dock.
Nov 29: Delivered to Klosters
R/A, Oslo. Passengers: 736.
Dec 21: First cruise, from Miami.
Cruising in Caribbean.
1985 All public rooms refitted by
350 staff from Lloydwerft,
Bremerhaven. They were flown to
Jacksonville, Florida, as
alternative to having ship out of
service for longer time while
making Atlantic crossings.
Passengers: 928.
Registered under the ownership of
K/S A/S Starward, Oslo.

1 Maksim Gorkiy, *flagship of the Soviet cruising fleet.* (Peter Voss.)
2 *At the time of her coming into service the* John Hamilton Gray *was counted as one of the world's largest ferries.* (CN Marine.)
3 *Klosters' first cruise liner, the* Starward, *berthed at Bremerhaven's Columbus Quay.* (Seebeckwerft.)

1

2

3

Motorship *Skyward*
K/S A/S Skyward, Oslo
PoR: Oslo

Builders: AG 'Weser', Werk
Seebeck, Bremerhaven
Yard no: 942
16,254 GRT; 2,110 DWT; 160.1 ×
22.8 m / 525 × 74.8 ft; Two 16-
cyl diesels, Maschinenfabrik
Augsburg-Nürnberg; Twin screw;
12,950 kW (17,380 BHP); 20 kn;
Passengers: 920; Crew: 250.

1969 Apr 27: 90 m (295 ft) long
after section launched.
Jun 28: Hull floated out of
building dock.
Dec 10: Delivered to Klosters
R/A, Oslo. Passengers: 750.
14-day Caribbean cruises from
Miami.
1984 Passengers: 920.
1985 Transferred to K/S A/S
Skyward, Oslo.

Motorship *Southward*
K/S A/S Southward, Oslo
PoR: Oslo

Builders: Cantieri Navali del
Tirreno e Riuniti, Riva Trigoso
Yard no: 288
16,607 GRT; 2,388 DWT; 163.4 ×
22.8 m / 536 × 74.8 ft; Four 10-
cyl geared diesels, FIAT; Twin
screw; 13,400 kW (18,000 BHP);
21.5 kn; Passengers: 918; Crew:
250.

1971 Jun 5: Launched.
Dec: Completed for Klosters R/A,
Oslo. Passengers: 750.
14-day Caribbean cruises from
Miami.
1984 Passengers: 918.
1985 Transferred to A/S K/S
Southward, Oslo.

Motorship *Song of Norway*
Royal Caribbean Cruise Line A/S,
Oslo
PoR: Oslo

Builders: O/Y Wärtsilä A/B,
Helsinki
Yard no: 392
23,005 GRT; 4,525 DWT; 194.3 ×
24.0 m / 637 × 78.7 ft; Four 9-cyl
geared diesels, Sulzer Bros-O/Y
Wärtsilä; Twin screw; 13,400 kW
(18,000 BHP); 20.5 kn;
Passengers: 1,196; Crew: 393.

1967 Dec 2: Launched.
1970 Oct 5: Delivered. Registered
under ownership of Sameiet ms
'Song of Norway', Oslo. 18,416
GRT. Length: 168.3 m (552 ft).
Passengers: 724. Crew: 320.
Nov 7: Maiden voyage, cruise
from Miami.
1978 Aug 30: Arrived at Helsinki
where lengthened by 26 m (85 ft).
Nov 26: Sailed for Miami
following completion of work.

1 *The* Skyward, *photographed at
Florida beneath a tropical sky.*
(Martin Lochte-Holtgreven.)
2 *The lines of the* Southward *still
appear almost futuristic.* (Martin
Lochte-Holtgreven.)
3 *The* Song of Norway *photographed
after she was lengthened in 1978.*
(Wärtsilä.)

1

2

3

Motorship *Nordic Prince*
Royal Caribbean Cruise Line A/S,
Oslo
PoR: Oslo

Builders: O/Y Wärtsilä A/B,
Helsinki
Yard no: 393
23,200 GRT; 3,700 DWT; 194.3 ×
24.0 m / 637 × 78.7 ft; Four 9-cyl
geared diesels, Sulzer Bros-O/Y
Wärtsilä; Twin screw; 13,400 kW
(18,000 BHP); 21 kn; Passengers:
1,194; Crew: 400.

1970 Jul 9: Launched.
1971 Jul 8: Delivered. Registered
under ownership of Sameiet ms
'Nordic Prince', Oslo. 18,436
GRT. Length: 168.3 m (552 ft).
Passengers: 714. Crew: 320.
Jul 31: First cruise, from Miami.
1980 Mar 7: Arrived at Helsinki
for lengthening.
Jun 17: Work completed.

Motorship *Sun Viking*
Royal Caribbean Cruise Line A/S,
Oslo
PoR: Oslo

Builders: O/Y Wärtsilä A/B,
Helsinki
Yard no: 394
18,559 GRT; 3,202 DWT; 171.7 ×
24.0 m / 563 × 78.7 ft; Four 9-cyl
geared diesels, Sulzer Bros-O/Y
Wärtsilä; Twin screw; 13,400 kW
(18,000 BHP); 21 kn; Passengers:
880; Crew: 320.

1971 Nov 27: Launched.
1972 Nov 10: Delivered.
Registered under ownership of
Sameiet ms 'Sun Viking', Oslo.
Dec 9: Maiden voyage, from
Miami to Caribbean.

Motorship *Kydon*
Anonymos Naftillaki Etaireia
Kritis AE, Canea
PoR: Canea

Ex *Wirakel*

Builders: NV Machinefabriek en
Scheepswerf van P. Smit, Jr,
Rotterdam
Yard no: 605
10,714 GRT; 153.9 × 20.0 m /505
× 65.6 ft; One 6-cyl diesel,
Burmeister & Wain-P. Smit;
Single screw; 4,125 kW (5,530
BHP); 14.25 kn; Passengers: 860.

1953 Mar 28: Launched as tanker
Wirakel for Phs. van Ommeren
NV, Rotterdam.
Jun: Completed for Suomen
Tankkilaiva O/Y, Helsinki. 9,583,
later 10,016 GRT.
1968 Purchased by Cretan
Maritime Co SA, Canea.
Renamed *Kydon*. Rebuilt as car
and passenger ferry. Registered
under ownership of Anonymos
Naftillaki Etaireia Kritis AE.
1970 Piraeus-Canea service.
1985 10,714 GRT.

1 *A striking view of the* Nordic Prince.
(Wärtsilä.)

2

2 *Sun Viking, the third ship of her class, has not so far been lengthened.* (Martin Lochte-Holtgreven.)

3 *The ferry* Kydon *began life as a tanker.* (Kludas collection.)

3

Motorship *Venus Venturer*
Pan Ocean Navigation Inc,
Panama
PoR: Panama

Ex *Scandinavian Sea*
Ex *Blenheim*

Builders: Upper Clyde
Shipbuilders Ltd, Clydebank
Division, Clydebank
Yard no: 744
10,736 GRT; 3,791 DWT; 149.4 ×
20.0 m / 490 × 65.6 ft; Two 18-
cyl geared diesels, Pielstick-
Crossley Premier Engines; Twin
screw; 13,400 kW (18,000 BHP);
22.5 kn; Passengers: 1,107.

1970 Jan 10: Launched as
Blenheim for Fred Olsen Lines
Ltd, London.
Sep 1: Delivered. 10,420 GRT.
Passengers: 396, on ferry service
995. Crew: 130. Private cars: 300.
Summer service between London
and Las Palmas. Cruising during
winter months.
1981 Sold to DFDS A/S
Copenhagen. Registered at
Nassau, Bahamas, under
ownership of DFDS Seacruises
(Bahamas) Ltd, Nassau.
Nov 1: Arrived at Hamburg for
refit by Blohm + Voss AG.
1982 Jan 18: Commissioned as
Scandinavian Sea.
Feb 12: First cruise from Miami to
Bahamas for 'Scandinavian World
Cruises'.
1984 Mar 9: During cruise from
Port Canaveral with 946
passengers a short circuit resulted
in an outbreak of fire in passenger
accommodation. Two lives lost
and heavy damage. Put back to
Port Canaveral. Declared total
loss.

May: Sold to Antonios Lelakis,
then to Panocean Navigation Inc,
Panama. Renamed *Venus
Venturer*. Managed by
Commodore Cruise Line.
1985 Feb 17: In tow of *Abeille
Provence* arrived at Valencia
where repaired.

Motorship *Pacific Princess*
P&O Lines Ltd (P&O Passenger
Division), London
PoR: London

Ex *Sea Venture*

Builders: Rheinstahl
Nordseewerke GmbH, Emden
Yard no: 411
20,636 GRT; 3,673 DWT; 168.7 ×
24.6 m / 553 × 80.7 ft; Four 10-
cyl geared diesels, FIAT; Twin
screw; 13,400 kW (18,000 BHP);
21.5 kn; Passengers: 600.

1970 May 9: Launched for
Norwegian Cruiseships A/S, Oslo.
1971 May 8: Shakedown cruise.
May 14: Christened *Sea Venture*
and delivered at Oslo. Registered
under ownership of K/S Sea
Venture A/S Co, Oslo. 19,903
GRT. Passengers: 767. Crew 317.
Jun: Maiden voyage, New York-
Hamilton cruise under
management of Flagship Cruises
Ltd, New York.
1972 Sep: Taken over by Oivind
Lorentzen A/S, Oslo, from
hitherto joint ownership: Oivind
Lorentzen A/S and Fearnley &
Eger A/S, Oslo.
1974 Oct: Sold to P&O Steam
Navigation Co, London, for
delivery April 1975.
1975 Apr: Renamed *Pacific
Princess*. Cruising from US ports,
in winter from Australian ports.
1985 20,636 GRT.

1 *The* Scandinavian Sea *was refitted
by Blohm + Voss for Caribbean
service.* (DFDS.)
2 *The* Pacific Princess. (Martin
Lochte-Holtgreven.)

1

2

Motorship *Island Princess*
P&O Lines Ltd (P&O Passenger
Division), London
PoR: London

Ex *Island Venture*

Builders: Rheinstahl
Nordseewerke GmbH, Emden
Yard no: 414
19,907 GRT; 3,390 DWT; 168.7 ×
24.6 m / 553 × 80.7 ft; Four 10-
cyl geared diesels, FIAT; Twin
screw; 13,400 kW (18,000 BHP);
21.5 kn; Passengers: 600.

1971 Mar 6: Launched for
Norwegian Cruiseships A/S, Oslo.
Nov 20: Trials.
Dec 14: Christened *Island Venture*
at Oslo. Passengers: 767. Crew:
317.
1972 Jan 4: Delivered.
Cruising, New York-Hamilton,
under management of Flagship
Cruises Ltd, New York.
Sep: To sole ownership of
Fearnley & Eger A/S, Oslo, from
hitherto joint ownership: Oivind
Lorentzen A/S, Oslo, and
Fearnley & Eger A/S. Renamed
Island Princess. Cruising from US
ports.
1974 Aug: Sold to P&O Steam
Navigation Co, London.
Continued cruising from US ports.

Motorship *Azur*
Nouvelle Cie de Paquebots,
Marseilles
PoR: Toulon

Ex *Eagle*

Builders: Dubigeon-Normandie
SA, Nantes
Yard no: 123
13,965 GRT; 2,085 DWT; 142.1 ×
22.6 m / 466 × 74.1 ft; Two 12-
cyl geared diesels, Pielstick-
Chantiers de l'Atlantique; Twin
screw; 16,300 kW (21,800 BHP);
23 kn; Passengers: 1,039.

1970 Oct 16: Launched as *Eagle*
for Southern Ferries (General
Steam Navigation Co Ltd),
London.
1971 Apr 22: Trials. 11,609 GRT.
Passengers: 740. Crew: 138.
Private cars: 200.
May 16: Delivered.
May 18: Maiden voyage
Southampton-Lisbon-Tangier.
1975 Oct: Sold to Nouvelle Cie de
Paquebots, Marseilles. Renamed
Azur. Ferry work and cruising in
Mediterranean.
1981 Rebuilt as cruiseship. 10,718
GRT. No provision for vehicles,
giving increased accommodation
for 1,039 passengers. Cruising in
Mediterranean from Toulon.
1983 14,717 GRT.
1984 13,965 GRT.

1 *The sister ship to the* Pacific
Princess, *the* Island Princess.
(Weirauch collection.)
2 *Since 1981 the former car ferry* Eagle
has served exclusively as a cruise-ship.
(Steffen Weirauch.)

Motorship *Princess of Acadia*
CN Marine Inc, Halifax/NS
PoR: St John

Builders: Saint John Shipbuilding
& Dry Dock Co Ltd, Saint John,
NB
Yard no: 98
10,051 GRT; 2,447 DWT; 146.3 ×
20.5 m / 480 × 67.3 ft; Four 16-
cyl geared diesels, General Motors
Corp; Twin screw; 8,550 kW
(11,500 BHP); 18.5 kn;
Passengers: 9, plus 641 unberthed;
Crew: 42; Private cars: 159.

1971 Launched as *Princess of
Nova*. Renamed before delivery.
May 15: Completed. 10,109 GRT.
May 27: Maiden voyage for
Canadian Pacific Ltd, Montreal,
PQ, New Brunswick-Nova Scotia
service.
1974 Sold to Canadian
Government.
1979 Registered under ownership
of CN Marine Inc, Halifax, NS.

Motorship *Scandinavian Star*
Stena A/B, Nassau, Bahamas
PoR: Nassau

Ex *Island Fiesta*
Ex *Stena Baltica*
Ex *Massalia*

Builders: Dubigeon-Normandie
SA, Nantes
Yard no: 124
10,513 GRT; 2,100 DWT; 141.8 ×
21.9 m / 465 × 71.9 ft; Two 16-
cyl geared diesels, Pielstick-
Chantiers de l'Atlantique; Twin
screw; 11,770 kW (15,780 BHP);
20 kn; Passengers: 494 1st class,
316 tourist class; Crew: 84; Private
cars: 260; Commercial vehicles:
36.

1971 Jan 19: Launched as
Massalia for Nouvelle Cie de
Paquebots, Marseilles.
Jul: Completed.
Marseilles-Casablanca-Canary
Islands service.
1984 Jan: Taken over by Stena
Cargo Line Ltd, Gothenburg.
Renamed *Stena Baltica*.
Nov: Renamed *Island Fiesta* for
intended service with
'Scandinavian World Cruises' of
DFDS A/S, Copenhagen.
Dec: Renamed again,
Scandinavian Star. Operating
between Tampa, Florida, and
Cozumel Island under Bahamian
flag.

1 *The* Princess of Acadia *in CN
Marine colours: blue hull and funnel,
white company device, gold band
around hull and bright blue-grey
superstructure.* (CN Marine.)
2 *The Mediterranean ferry* Massalia.
(Jean M. Otten.)

Motorship *Sunward II*
K/S A/S Sunward II, Oslo
PoR: Oslo

Ex *Cunard Adventurer*

Builders: Rotterdamsche
Droogdok Maats NV, Rotterdam
Yard no: 329
14,110 GRT; 2,314 DWT; 148.1 ×
21.6 m / 486 × 70.9 ft; Four 12-
cyl geared diesels, Stork-
Werkspoor; Twin screw; 20,150
kW (27,000 BHP); 21.5 kn;
Passengers: 857.

1971 Feb 2: Launched as *Cunard
Adventurer* for Cunard-ONA Ltd,
Southampton. Originally ordered
by Overseas National Airways Inc
in which Cunard had 50 per cent
share. In July 1970 Cunard
acquired balance of equity of
ONA.
Aug 28: Trials. 14,151 GRT.
Passengers: 832. Crew: 412.
Oct 19: Delivered.
Nov 19: Maiden voyage
Southampton-San Juan.
Caribbean cruising.
1976 Registered under ownership
of Cunard Cruise Ships Ltd, New
York.
1977 Sold to Klosters R/A, Oslo.
Renamed *Sunward II*.
Mar 8: Arrived at Bremerhaven
for alterations at yard of Hapag-
Lloyd AG.
Apr 24: Work completed. 14,110
GRT. Caribbean cruising.
1984 Passengers: 857.
1985 Transferred to K/S A/S
Sunward II, Oslo.

Motorship *Royal Viking Star*
Norwegian Caribbean Lines A/S,
Oslo
PoR: Bergen

Builders: O/Y Wärtsilä A/B,
Helsinki
Yard no: 395
28,221 GRT; 5,656 DWT; 205.5 ×
25.2 m / 674 × 82.7 ft; Four 9-cyl
geared diesels from builders; Twin
screw; 13,400 kW (18,000 BHP);
18.5, max 21 kn; Passengers: 812.

1971 May 12: Launched.
1972 Jun 26: Delivered. Owners:
Det Bergenske D/S, Bergen.
21,847 GRT. Length: 177.7 m
(583 ft). Passengers: 539. Crew:
326.
Worldwide cruising.
1981 Aug 30: Arrived at AG
'Weser' Seebeckwerft,
Bremerhaven, where lengthened
by fitting of 27.7 m (91 ft)
prefabricated amidships section.
Nov 22: Delivered upon
completion of work. 28,221 GRT.
1984 May: Agreement in principle
for purchase of K/S Royal Viking
Line A/S by US investor group
headed by J.H. Whitney & Co.
Aug: Did not proceed. Royal
Viking Line, three ships and
organisations in US and Norway
purchased by Norwegian
Caribbean Lines, Oslo.
Passengers: 812.

1

2

1 *Following their purchase of the* Sunward II *Klosters had her exterior brought into line with the appearance of other cruise-ships in their fleet.* (Norwegian Caribbean Lines.)

2 *In 1981* Royal Viking Star *was the first of the three sister ships to be lengthened.* (Peter Voss.)

Motorship *Royal Viking Sky*
Norwegian Caribbean Lines A/S,
Oslo
PoR: Trondheim

Builders: O/Y Wärtsilä A/B,
Helsinki
Yard no: 396
28,078 GRT; 5,660 DWT; 205.5 ×
25.2 m / 674 × 82.7 ft; Four 9-cyl
geared diesels, Sulzer Bros-O/Y
Wärtsilä; Twin screw; 13,400 kW
(18,000 BHP); 18.5, max 21 kn;
Passengers: 812.

1972 May 25: Launched.
1973 Jun 5: Delivered. Owners:
Det Nordenfjeldske D/S,
Trondheim. 21,891 GRT. Length:
177.7 m (583 ft). Passengers: 536.
Crew: 324.
Worldwide cruising.
1982 Sep 10: Arrived at AG
'Weser' Seebeckwerft,
Bremerhaven, where lengthened
by fitting of 27.7 m (91 ft)
prefabricated amidships section.
Nov 27: Delivered upon
completion of work. 28,078 GRT.
1984 May: Agreement in principle
for purchase of K/S Royal Viking
Line A/S by US investor group
headed by J.H. Whitney & Co.
Aug: Did not proceed. Royal
Viking Line, three ships and
organisations in US and Norway
purchased by Norwegian
Caribbean Lines, Oslo.
Passengers: 812.

Motorship *Royal Viking Sea*
Norwegian Caribbean Lines A/S,
Oslo
PoR: Oslo

Builders: O/Y Wärtsilä A/B,
Helsinki
Yard no: 397
28,018 GRT; 5,660 DWT; 205.5 ×
25.2 m / 674 × 82.7 ft; Four 9-cyl
geared diesels, Sulzer Bros-O/Y
Wärtsilä; Twin screw; 13,400 kW
(18,000 BHP); 18.5, max 21 kn;
Passengers: 812.

1973 Jan 19: Launched.
Nov 16: Delivered. Owners: A.F.
Klaveness & Co A/S, Lysaker.
21,848 GRT. Length: 177.7 m (583
ft). Passengers: 536. Crew: 324.
Nov 25: Maiden voyage, Bergen-
Newcastle service, temporarily
replacing *Leda* during overhaul.
Dec: Worldwide cruising.
1983 Mar 11: Arrived at AG
'Weser' Seebeckwerft,
Bremerhaven, where lengthened
by fitting of 27.7 m (91 ft)
prefabricated amidships section.
Jun 5: Delivered upon completion
of work. 28,018 GRT.
Nov 29: Rescued 151 survivors
from Indian ferry *Dojo* adrift 11
days in Celebes Sea.
1984 May: Agreement in principle
for purchase of K/S Royal Viking
Line A/S by US investor group
headed by J.H. Whitney & Co.
Aug: Did not proceed. Royal
Viking Line, three ships and
organisations in US and Norway
purchased by Norwegian
Caribbean Lines, Oslo.
Passengers: 812.

Motorship *Sun Flower*
Taiyo Ferry KK, Kanda
PoR: Kanda

Builders: Kawasaki Heavy
Industries Ltd, Kobe
Yard no: 1158
12,130 GRT; 3,243 DWT; 185.7 ×
24.0 m / 609 × 78.7 ft; Four 12-
cyl geared diesels,
Maschinenfabrik Augsburg-
Nürnberg-Kawasaki Heavy
Industries; Twin screw; 19,500 kW
(26,080 BHP); 24 kn; Passengers:
1,124; Crew: 87; Private cars: 208;
Commercial vehicles: 84.

1971 Sep 8: Launched.
1972 Jan 18: Delivered to Nippon
Kosoku Ferry KK, Tokyo. 12,116
GRT.
Feb 1: Maiden voyage Nagoya-
Kagoshima.
1978 Owners: Taiyo Ferry KK,
Kanda.
1983 Jun: 12,130 GRT.

1 *The* Royal Viking Sky *after her
lengthening at the Seebeck yard.*
(Peter Voss.)
2 *As the last of the three ships to have
been rebuilt, the* Royal Viking Sea *left
Bremerhaven in June 1983.* (Peter
Voss.)
3 *The* Sun Flower, *prototype of a
successful series of ferries.*
(Kawasaki.)

1

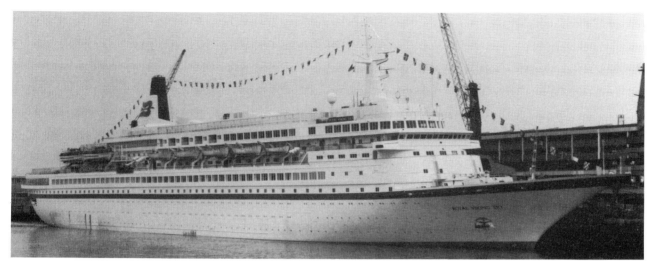

2

3

Motorship *Sun Flower 2*
Osaka Shosen Mitsu Senpaku KK,
Osaka
PoR: Osaka

Builders: Kawasaki Heavy
Industries Ltd, Kobe
Yard no: 1159
12,104 GRT; 3,317 DWT; 185.7 ×
24.0 m / 609 × 78.7 ft; Four 12-
cyl geared diesels,
Maschinenfabrik Augsburg-
Nürnberg-Kawasaki Heavy
Industries; Twin screw; 19,500 kW
(26,080 BHP); 24 kn; Passengers:
1,124; Crew: 87; Private cars: 208;
Commercial vehicles: 84.

1972 Jan 18: Launched as *Sun
Rise* for Nippon Kosoku Ferry
KK, Tokyo.
May 17: Delivered as *Sun Flower
2*. 12,090 GRT. Passengers: 1,378.
May 28: Maiden voyage Nagoya-
Kagoshima.
1978 Owners: Taiyo Ferry KK,
Kanda.
1983 Sold to Osaka Shosen Mitsu
Senpaku KK, Osaka. 12,104
GRT. Passengers: 1,124.

Motorship *Sun Flower 5*
Nippon Kosoku Ferry KK, Tokyo
PoR: Tokyo

Builders: Kurushima Dock Co
Ltd, Imabari
Yard no: 730
13,321 GRT; 3,231 DWT; 185.0 ×
24.0 m / 607 × 78.7 ft; Four 12-
cyl geared diesels,
Maschinenfabrik Augsburg-
Nürnberg-Kawasaki Heavy
Industries; Twin screw; 19,450 kW
(26,080 BHP); 24 kn; Passengers:
1,079; Crew: 87; Private cars: 92;
Commercial vehicles: 100.

1973 Mar 3: Completed. 12,711
GRT.
Mar 21: Maiden voyage Tokio-
Kochi.
1978 13,334 GRT.
1982 13,338 GRT following refit.
1984 13,321 GRT.

Motorship *Sun Flower 8*
Nippon Kosoku Ferry KK, Tokyo
PoR: Tokyo

Builders: Kurushima Dock Co
Ltd, Imabari
Yard no: 731
12,771 GRT; 3,280 DWT; 185.0 ×
24.0 m / 607 × 78.7 ft; Four 12-
cyl geared diesels,
Maschinenfabrik Augsburg-
Nürnberg-Kawasaki Heavy
Industries; Twin screw; 19,500 kW
(26,080 BHP); 24 kn; Passengers:
1,079; Crew: 87; Private cars: 92;
Commercial vehicles: 100.

1973 Jun 25: Launched.
Jul 4: Maiden voyage Tokyo-
Kochi.
1983 12,771 GRT.

1 *Like her sister ship* Sun Flower, *the*
Sun Flower 2 *has operated since 1978
for Tokyo Ferries.* (Kawasaki.)
2 Sun Flower 5 *at full speed.* (Kludas
collection.)
3 Sun Flower 8: (Yoshitatsu Fukawa.)

1

2

3

Motorship *Shin Sakura Maru*
Mitsui OSK Lines Ltd, Tokyo
PoR: Osaka

Builders: Mitsubishi Heavy
Industries Ltd, Kobe
Yard no: 1033
16,431 GRT; 4,700 DWT; 175.8 ×
24.6 m / 577 × 80.7 ft; One 8-cyl
diesel from builders; Single screw;
16,100 kW (21,600 BHP); 21.3 kn;
Passengers: 552; Crew: 79.

1971 Dec 18: Launched.
1972 Jul 18: Delivered to Nihon
Sangyo Junko Mihonichi Kyokai,
Tokyo. Passengers: 92.
Jul 27: Maiden voyage Tokyo-
Europe as exhibition ship for
Japanese industry. When not so
used, on Mitsui OSK Lines Ltd
service Japan-America and other
routes, from 1973 without
passengers.
1980 Dec: Sold to Mitsui OSK
Lines Ltd, Tokyo.
1981 Aug-Dec: Rebuilt by
Mitsubishi Heavy Industries Ltd
as cruise ship for school children
and students. 16,431 GRT.
1982 Cruising in Pacific.

Motorship *Fabiolaville*
Cie Maritime Belge SA, Antwerp
PoR: Antwerp

Builders: Cockerill Yards
Hoboken SA, NV, Hoboken
Yard no: 861
13,303 GRT; 15,349 DWT; 161.1
× 23.1 m / 529 × 75.8 ft; One
8-cyl diesel, Burmeister & Wain-
Cockerill; Single screw; 11,200 kW
(15,040 BHP); 20 kn; Passengers:
71; Crew: 58.

1972 Jan 28: Launched.
May 15-18: Trials. 13,481 GRT.
Jun 2: Delivered.
Hamburg-Antwerp-Matadi
service. Currently from Antwerp
only.
1983 13,303 GRT.

Motorship *Kananga*
Cie Maritime Zaîroise, Kinshasa
PoR: Matadi

Builders: Cockerill Yards
Hoboken SA, NV, Hoboken
Yard no: 862
13,481 GRT; 15,350 DWT; 161.2
× 23.1 m / 529 × 75.8 ft; One 8-
cyl diesel, Burmeister & Wain-
Cockerill; Single screw; 11,200 kW
(15,040 BHP); 19 kn; Passengers:
71; Crew: 58.

1972 Aug 24: Launched.
1973 Jan 29-Feb 1: Trials.
Feb 9: Delivered.
Feb 15: Maiden voyage Antwerp-
Matadi.
1975 Nov 15: In collision with
Soviet trawler *Youzas Garyalis*
west of Ile de Seine. Passengers
and part of crew taken off and
Kananga brought into Brest by tug
Baltic on November 16.

1

2

3

1 *With her superstructure extended forward, following her 1981 refit the* Shin Sakura Maru *has an even more distinctive appearance than before.* (Yoshitatsu Fukawa.)
2 *The* Fabiolaville *is one of the few remaining passenger liners operating from Europe on regular services.* (Weirauch collection.)
3 *Until 1983 the* Kananga *was the largest African passenger ship.* (Rudie Kleyn.)

Motorship *Sun Princess*
P&O Lines Ltd, London
PoR: London

Ex *Spirit of London*

Builders: Cantieri Navali del
Tirreno e Riuniti, Riva Trigoso
Yard no: R 290
17,370 GRT; 2,352 DWT; 163.3 ×
22.8 m / 536 × 74.8 ft; Four 10-
cyl geared diesels, FIAT; Twin
screw; 13,450 kW (18,000 BHP);
20.5 kn; Passengers: 700.

1972 Apr 9: Launched as *Spirit of
London*.
Originally ordered by Klosters
R/A, Oslo. Contract taken over
by P&O in 1971.
Aug: Completed.
Sep: Delivered.
Nov 11: Maiden voyage
Southampton-San Juan. Cruising,
US West Coast.
1974 Oct: Renamed *Sun Princess*.

Motorship *Bolero*
Fred Olsen & Co, Oslo
PoR: Oslo

Ex *Scandinavica*
Ex *Bolero*

Builders: Dubigeon-Normandie
SA, Nantes
Yard no: 133
10,568 GRT; 1,829 DWT; 141.5 ×
21.9 m / 464 × 71.9 ft; Two 12-
cyl geared diesels, Pielstick-
Chantiers de l'Atlantique; Twin
screw; 14,200 kW (20,400 BHP);
21 kn; Passengers: 872 berthed,
728 unberthed; Crew: 84; Private
cars: 400.

1972 Jun 13: Launched.
1973 Feb: Completed. 11,344
GRT.
Did not take up service between
Travemünde and Södertälje for
which ordered. On Prinzen Linien
service Bremerhaven/Hamburg-
Harwich before transfer to US for
service Portland-Yarmouth.
Cruising in winter.
1976 Oct: Newcastle-Oslo service.
1978 Apr: Chartered to Stena Line
A/B, Gothenburg. Renamed
Scandinavica. Gothenburg-Kiel
service.
1981 Plan for use by Brittany
Ferries as *Tregor* not
implemented. Converted by
Frederikshavns Vaerft & Flydedok
A/S, Frederikshavn, to carry
1,600 passengers and 400 private
cars.
1982 Renamed *Bolero*.
Sep 23: First voyage Hirtshals-
Stavanger-Bergen service.
1983 May 3: Between Stavanger
and Kristiansand fire broke out on
car deck. Passengers transferred to
other vessels. One passenger died.

Returned to service following
repairs by Blohm + Voss AG,
Hamburg.

1 The Sun Princess *off San Francisco
in 1981.* (Weirauch collection.)
2 *Following voyages under charter on
various European and American
routes, the* Bolero *is now operating
again under Olsen house colours.*
(Achim Borchert.)

Motorship *Odessa*
Black Sea Shipping Co, Odessa
PoR: Odessa

Ex *Copenhagen*

Builders: Vickers Ltd, Barrow
Yard no: 1085
13,253 GRT; 2,137 DWT; 136.3 ×
21.5 m / 447 × 70.5 ft; Two 16-
cyl geared diesels, Pielstick-
Crossley Premier Engines; Twin
screw; 11,950 kW (16,000 BHP);
19 kn; Passengers: 590.

1970 Laid down to order of K/S
Nordline A/S, Copenhagen.
Nov: Incomplete ship advertised
for sale on stocks because of
differences between shipping
company and builders over
acceptance of considerable extra
costs.
1971 Sep: Agreement between K/S
Nordline A/S and Vickers Ltd that
building of ship should proceed.
Intended name was *Prinz Henrik
af Danmark*.
1972 Dec 20: Launched unnamed.
1973 Mar 27: Towed from Barrow
to Newcastle where ship completed
by Swan Hunter Shipbuilders Ltd.
1974 Mar: First trials. 13,758
GRT.
Apr: K/S Nordline A/S, placed
Copenhagen on sale list.
1975 May: Sold to Soviet Union,
Black Sea Shipping Co, Odessa.
Renamed *Odessa*.
Jul 18: Handing over voyage,
Liverpool-Leningrad. Cruising.
1983 13,253 GRT.

Motorship *Ferry Akashia*
Shin Nipponkai Ferry KK, Osaka
PoR: Otaru

Builders: Kanda Zosensho KK,
Kure
Yard no: 178
11,210 GRT; 4,173 DWT; 180.5 ×
26.5 m / 592 × 86.9 ft; Two 16-
cyl geared diesels,
Maschinenfabrik Augsburg-
Nürnberg-Kawasaki Heavy
Industries; Twin screw; 23,900 kW
(32,000 BHP); 23 kn; Passengers:
1,387; Private cars: 150;
Commercial vehicles: 119.

1973 Mar 1: Launched.
Jul 14: Delivered.
Jul 21: Maiden voyage, Tsuruga-
Otaru ferry service.

1 Odessa *off Bremerhaven in June
1985.* (Peter Voss.)
2 *In common with many Japanese
ferries, the* Ferry Akashia *presents a
distinctive profile.* (Kludas collection.)

1

2

Motorship *Dana Regina*
DFDS A/S, Copenhagen
PoR: Esbjerg

Builders: Aalborg Vaerft A/S, Aalborg
Yard no: 200
11,996 GRT; 2,836 DWT; 153.7 × 22.4 m / 504 × 73.5 ft; Four 8-cyl geared diesels, Burmeister & Wain-Helsingör Skibsvaerft; Twin screw; 13,130 kW (17,600 BHP); 21.5 kn; Passengers: 1,006; Crew: 185; Private cars: 250; Commercial vehicles: 100.

1973 Aug 31: Launched unnamed.
1974 Jul 1: Named and delivered. Cruise to London.
Jul 9: Maiden voyage, Esbjerg-Harwich service.
1983 Oct: Copenhagen-Oslo service.

Motorship *Norland*
North Sea Ferries Ltd, Hull
PoR: Hull

Builders: AG 'Weser', Werk Seebeck, Bremerhaven
Yard no: 972
12,988 GRT; 4,036 DWT; 153.0 × 24.7 m / 502 × 81.0 ft; Two 16-cyl geared diesels, Stork-Werkspoor; Twin screw; 13,430 kW (18,000 BHP); 19 kn; Passengers: 1,072, plus 173 unberthed; Crew: 98.

1973 Oct 13: Launched.
1974 Jun 7: Delivered.
Ferry service Hull-Rotterdam.
1982 Apr 17: Requisitioned by British Government for use as transport in Falklands war.
1983 Jan: Released from government service.
Apr 1: Following overhaul returned to Hull-Rotterdam service.

Motorship *Norstar*
Noordzee Veerdiensten BV, Rotterdam
PoR: Rotteram

Builders: AG 'Weser', Werk Seebeck, Bremerhaven
Yard no: 973
12,502 GRT; 4,578 DWT; 153.0 × 24.7 m / 502 × 81.0 ft; Two 16-cyl geared diesels, Stork-Werkspoor; Twin screw; 13,430 kW (18,000 BHP); 18.5 kn; Passengers: 1,070, plus 173 unberthed; Crew: 98.

1974 Jul 5: Launched.
Dec 14: Delivered.
Ferry service Rotterdam-Hull.

1

1 *The lines of the* Dana Regina *have a classical elegance.* (Skyfotos.)
2 *The* Norland *was another unit of the British Task Force sent to the Falklands in 1982.* (Kludas collection.)
3 *The* Norstar *approaching her Rotterdam terminal.* (Achim Borchert.)

2

3

Motorship *Tassili*
Soc Nationale de Transport
Maritime & Cie Nationale
Algérienne de Navigation
Maritime (SNTM/CNAN),
Algiers
PoR: Algiers

Ex *Central No. 1*

Builders: Mitsubishi Heavy
Industries Ltd, Shimonoseki
Yard no: 688
10,233 GRT; 2,500 DWT; 130.4 ×
22.0 m / 428 × 72.2 ft; Two 9-cyl
diesels from builders; Twin screw;
11,200 kW (15,000 BHP); 19.5 kn;
Passengers: 59 1st class, 416 2nd
class, 80 commercial vehicle
drivers, 300 unberthed; Private
cars: 20; Commercial vehicles:
130.

1970 Nov 14: Launched as *Central
No. 1*.
1971 Mar 29: Delivered to Central
Ferry Co Ltd, Kobe. 5,744 GRT.
Kobe-Tokyo service.
1973 Bought by Cie Nationale
Algérienne de Navigation
(CNAN), Algiers. Renamed
Tassili. Marseilles-Algiers-Oran
service.
1974 10,233 GRT.
1984 Owners Soc Nationale de
Transport Maritime & Cie
Nationale Algérienne de
Navigation Maritime
(SNTM/CNAN), Algiers.

Motorship *El-Djazair*
Soc Nationale de Transport
Maritime & Cie Nationale
Algérienne de Navigation
Maritime (SNTM/CNAN),
Algiers
PoR: Algiers

Ex *Central No. 3*

Builders: Kanasashi Zosensho,
Shimizu
Yard no: 965
12,124 GRT; 2,893 DWT; 130.4 ×
22.0 m / 428 × 72.2 ft; Two 14-
cyl geared diesels,
Maschinenfabrik Augsburg-
Nürnberg-Kawasaki Heavy
Industries; Twin screw; 11,350 kW
(15,200 BHP); 19.5 kn;
Passengers: 500, plus 300
unberthed; Private cars: 22;
Commercial vehicles: 99.

1971 Mar 26: Launched as *Central
No. 3* for Central Ferry Co Ltd,
Kobe.
Jul 22: Delivered. 5,647 GRT.
1973 Bought by Cie Nationale
Algérienne de Navigation
(CNAN), Algiers. Renamed *El-
Djazair*. Marseilles-Algiers-Oran
service.
1974 12,529 GRT.
1975 11,602 GRT, since 1976
12,124 GRT.
1984 Owners Soc Nationale de
Transport Maritime & Cie
Nationale Algérienne de
Navigation Maritime
(SNTM/CNAN), Algiers.

1 *The* Tassili *at the entrance to
Marseilles harbour in 1977.* (Arnold
Kludas.)
2 *The largest Algerian ferry, the* El-
Djezair. (R.K. Elber.)

Motorship *Belorussiya*
Black Sea Shipping Co, Odessa
PoR: Odessa

Builders: O/Y Wärtsilä A/B, Åbo
Yard no: 1212
13,251 GRT; 2,251 DWT; 156.2 ×
21.8 m / 512 × 71.5 ft; Two 18-
cyl geared diesels, Pielstick-O/Y
Wärtsilä; Twin screw; 13,430 kW
(18,000 BHP); 21.25 kn;
Passengers: 504, plus 505
unberthed, 350 when cruising;
Crew: 191; Private cars: 256;
Commercial vehicles: 23.

1974 Mar 6: Launched.
1975 Jan 15: Delivered. 16,631
GRT.
Cruising in European waters.
1980 13,251 GRT.

Motorship *Gruziya*
Black Sea Shipping Co, Odessa
PoR: Odessa

Builders: O/Y Wärtsilä A/B, Åbo
Yard no: 1213
13,252 GRT; 3,004 DWT; 156.3 ×
21.8 m / 513 × 71.5 ft; Two 18-
cyl geared diesels, Pielstick-O/Y
Wärtsilä; Twin screw; 13,430 kW
(18,000 BHP); 21 kn; Passengers:
650, plus 110 unberthed; 350 when
cruising; Crew: 191; Private cars:
256; Commercial vehicles: 23.

1974 Oct 18: Launched.
1975 Jun 30: Delivered. 16,331
GRT. Passengers: 504, plus 505
unberthed.
Mainly cruising in European
waters.
1980 13,251 GRT.
1984 13,252 GRT. Passengers:
650, plus 110 unberthed.

1 *The Soviet 'Belorussiya' class, of
which the prototype ship is illustrated,
have successfully established
themselves in the European cruising
market.* (Peter Voss.)
2 *In 1980, through taking advantage
of the measurement rules, the ships of
the 'Belorussiya' class became each
about 3,000 gross registered tons
smaller. The photograph shows the
Gruziya.* (Alex Duncan.)

Motorship *Azerbaydzhan*
Black Sea Shipping Co, Odessa
PoR: Odessa

Builders: O/Y Wärtsilä A/B, Åbo
Yard no: 1221
13,252 GRT; 2,251 DWT; 156.2 ×
21.8 m / 512 × 71.5 ft; Two 18-
cyl geared diesels, Pielstick-O/Y
Wärtsilä; Twin screw; 13,430 kW
(18,000 BHP); 21.5 kn;
Passengers: 650, plus 110
unberthed, 350 when cruising;
Crew: 191; Private cars: 256;
Commercial vehicles: 23.

1975 Apr 14: Launched.
Dec 18: Delivered. 16,631 GRT.
Passengers: 505, plus 505
unberthed.
Mainly cruising.
1978 13,251 GRT.
1984 13,252 GRT. Passengers:
650, plus 110 unberthed.

Motorship *Kazakhstan*
Black Sea Shipping Co, Odessa
PoR: Odessa

Builders: O/Y Wärtsilä A/B, Åbo
Yard no: 1222
13,252 GRT; 2,402 DWT; 156.3 ×
21.8 m / 513 × 71.5 ft; Two 18-
cyl geared diesels, Pielstick-O/Y
Wärtsilä; Twin screw; 13,430 kW
(18,000 BHP); 20 kn; Passengers:
650, plus 110 unberthed, 500 when
cruising; Crew: 250; Private
cars: 256; Commercial vehicles:
23.

1975 Oct 17: Launched.
1976 Jun: Delivered. 16,631 GRT.
Passengers: 504, plus 505
unberthed.
Mainly cruising.
1980 13,251 GRT.
1984 Feb 8-May 9: Reconstructed
by Lloydwerft, Bremerhaven, to
Western European standards. 79
new cabins, increasing capacity to
500 passengers. Crew: 250. 13,252
GRT.

1 *The* Azerbaydzhan *turning in the
Weser.* (Ralf Witthohn.)
2 *The* Kazakhstan *beneath the slopes
of Geiranger Fjord.* (Peter Voss.)

Motorship *Leonid Brezhnev*
Black Sea Shipping Co, Odessa
PoR: Odessa

Ex *Kareliya*

Builders: O/Y Wärtsilä A/B, Åbo
Yard no: 1223
13,252 GRT; 2,402 DWT; 156.3 ×
21.8 m / 513 × 71.5 ft; Two 18-
cyl geared diesels, Pielstick-O/Y
Wärtsilä; Twin screw; 13,430 kW
(18,000 BHP); 21 kn; Passengers:
650, plus 50 unberthed, 350 when
cruising; Crew: 191; Private cars:
256; Commercial vehicles: 23.

1976 Apr 14: Launched as
Kareliya.
Dec: Delivered. 16,631 GRT.
Passengers: 504, plus 505
unberthed.
Mainly cruising.
1980 13,251 GRT.
1981 Jun 1: Ran aground off
Arrecife, Canary Islands, on
cruise from London. So badly
damaged that passengers had to be
disembarked and flown home.
Jul 30: Arrived in Tyne where
repaired and facilities for
passengers thoroughly overhauled.
1982 Dec: Renamed *Leonid
Brezhnev*.
1984 13,252 GRT. Passengers:
650, plus 50 unberthed.

Motorship *Sapporo Maru*
Nippon Enkai Ferry KK, Tokyo
PoR: Tokyo

Builders: Hayashikane Zosen KK,
Shimonoseki
Yard no: 1177
11,097 GRT; 4,213 DWT; 164.0 ×
24.0 m / 538 × 78.7 ft; Two 14-
cyl diesels, Maschinenfabrik
Augsburg-Nürnberg-Mitsubishi
Heavy Industries; Twin screw;
20,900 kW (28,000 BHP); 22.25
kn; Passengers: 808.

1974 Apr 9: Launched.
Jul: Completed.
Aug 2: Maiden voyage Tokyo-
Tomakomei.

Motorship *Sun Flower 11*
Nippon Kosuku Ferry KK, Tokyo
PoR: Tokyo

Builders: Kurushima Dock Co
Ltd, Onishi
Yard no: 775
13,575 GRT; 3,110 DWT; 195.8 ×
24.0 m / 642 × 78.7 ft; Two 18-
cyl diesels, Maschinenfabrik
Augsburg-Nürnberg-Kawasaki
Heavy Industries; Twin screw;
26,900 kW (36,000 BHP); 25 kn;
Passengers: 1,218; Crew: 87;
Private cars: 192; Commercial
vehicles: 85.

1974 Apr 23: Launched.
Sep 9: Delivered. 13,598 GRT.
Osaka-Kagoshima ferry service.
1982 13,575 GRT following refit.

1 *The* Kareliya *at Las Palmas in 1982.
Following the death of the Soviet head
of state she was renamed* Leonid
Brezhnev. *(Peter Voss.)*
2 *The ferry* Sapporo Maru. *(Stephen
Kentwell.)*
3 *The two-funneller among the car
ferries,* Sun Flower 11. *(Stephen
Kentwell.)*

1

2

3

Motorship *Pegasus*
Cosmos Cruises Maritime Co,
Piraeus
PoR: Piraeus

Ex *Sundancer*
Ex *Svea Corona*

Builders: Dubigeon-Normandie
SA, Nantes
Yard no: 141
12,576 GRT; 1,746 DWT; 153.1 ×
22.3 m / 502 × 73.2 ft; Four 12-
cyl geared diesels, Pielstick-
Chantiers de l'Atlantique; Twin
screw; 17,900 kW (24,000 BHP);
22 kn; Crew 150; Private cars:
290.
1974 Jul 19: Launched as *Svea
Corona*.
1975 Delivered to Stockholms
Rederi A/B Svea, Stockholm.
Passengers: 799, plus 401
unberthed.
Helsinki-Stockholm service.
1981 Rederi A/B Svea taken over
by Johnson Line A/B, Stockholm.
1984 Vessel transferred to
Sundance Cruises, formed by
Johnson Line A/B, Stockholm;
Finska Angfartygs A/B (EFFOA),
Helsinki; and McDonald
Industries, Seattle. Converted at
Oskarshamn to cruiseship by Nya
Oskarshamns Varv A/B.
Renamed *Sundancer*. Bahamian
flag.
Jun: Ashore at Duncan Bay,
Vancouver. Badly damaged.
Aug: Refloated. Towed to
Vancouver. Heavy third-party
claim in respect of damaged dock.
Nov: Sold to Epirotiki Lines SA,
Piraeus. Renamed *Pegasus*.
1985 Jan 22: Arrived at Piraeus in
tow of *Suhaili,* to be rebuilt.
Owners recorded as Cosmos
Cruises Maritime Co, Piraeus.

1986 May: Cruising between
Vancouver and Alaska.

Motorship *Dana Gloria*
DFDS A/S, Copenhagen
PoR: Esbjerg

Ex *Svea Corona*
Ex *Dana Gloria*
Ex *Wellamo*

Builders: Dubigeon-Normandie
SA, Nantes
Yard no: 142
12,348 GRT; 1,719 DWT; 153.1 ×
22.3 m / 502 × 73.2 ft; Four 12-
cyl geared diesels, Pielstick-
Chantiers de l'Atlantique; Twin
screw; 17,900 kW (24,000 BHP);
22 kn; Passengers: 799, plus 401
unberthed; Crew: 150; Private
cars: 290.

1974 Nov: Launched as *Wellamo*
for Finska Angfartygs A/B,
Helsinki.
1975 Delivered.
Helsinki-Stockholm service.
1979 Sold to DFDS A/S,
Copenhagen, with delivery 1981.
1981 May: *Dana Gloria* of DFDS
A/S. Esbjerg-Newcastle service.
1983 Copenhagen-Oslo service.
1984 Renamed *Svea Corona*.
1985 Renamed *Dana Gloria*.

1 *The* Svea Corona–*subsequently
renamed* Sundancer *and* Pegasus–*with
Johnson Line funnel colours.* (K.
Brzoza.)
2 *Since 1981 the* Dana Gloria *has sailed
for DFDS.* (DFDS.)

1

2

Motorship *Orient Express*
Baldur Ltd (Sea Management
Services SMS) (Sealink UK Ltd)
PoR: Hamilton

Ex *Silja Star*
Ex *Bore Star*

Builders: Dubigeon-Normandie
SA, Nantes
Yard no: 143
12,343 GRT; 1,880 DWT; 153.1 ×
22.3 m / 502 × 73.2 ft; Four 12-
cyl geared diesels, Pielstick-
Chantiers de l'Atlantique; Twin
screw; 17,900 kW (24,000 BHP);
22 kn; Passengers: 799, plus 401
unberthed; Crew: 150; Private
cars: 290.

1975 Jan 30: Launched as *Bore
Star* for Angfartygs A/B Bore,
Åbo.
Dec: Delivered.
Dec 11: Maiden cruise, France to
West Africa and return to
Cherbourg. Thereafter Helsinki-
Stockholm service.
1980 To Finska Angfartygs A/B as
Silja Star.
1985 Nov: Sold for service with
Sealink UK Ltd. Renamed *Orient
Express*.

1986 Temporary charter to Club
Sea Inc for Caribbean cruising.
Renamed *Club Sea*.

Motorship *Ishikari*
Taiheiyo Enkai Ferry KK, Nagoya
PoR: Nagoya

Builders: Nakai Zosen KK, Setoda
Yard no: 387
12,853 GRT; 5,422 DWT; 188.4 ×
24.0 m / 618 × 78.7 ft; Two 14-
cyl diesels, Maschinenfabrik
Augsburg-Nürnberg-Mitsubishi
Heavy Industries; Twin screw;
20,580 kW (27,580 BHP); 21.5 kn;
Passengers: 905.

1974 Sep 19: Launched.
Dec 23: Delivered. Length then
175.6 m / 576 ft. 11,880 GRT. 23
kn. Private cars: 105. Commercial
vehicles: 130.
Nagoya-Ohita (Kyushu) service.
1975 Nagoya-Sendai-Tomakomai
service.
1981 Lengthened by 12.8 m / 42
ft.

Motorship *Daisetsu*
Taiheiyo Enkai Ferry KK, Nagoya
PoR: Nagoya

Builders: Nakai Zosen KK, Setoda
Yard no: 388
12,854 GRT; 5,432 DWT; 188.4 ×
24.0 m / 618 × 78.7 ft; Two 14-
cyl diesels, Maschinenfabrik
Augsburg-Nürnberg-Mitsubishi
Heavy Industries; Twin screw;
20,580 kW (27,580 BHP); 21.5 kn;
Passengers: 905.

1975 Mar 28: Launched.
Jun 20: Delivered. Length then
175.6 m / 576 ft. Private cars: 105.
Commercial vehicles: 130.
Nagoya-Sendai-Tomokomai
service.
1980 Lengthened by 12.8 m /
42 ft.

1 *The former* Silja Star *under her new
name* Orient Express. (Peter Voss.)
2 *The* Ishikari, *lengthened by
12.8 m (42 ft) between bridge structure
and funnel.* (Nakai Zosen.)
3 *The* Daisetsu *before she was rebuilt
like her sister ship.* (Nakai Zosen.)

1

2

3

Motorship *Tor Britannia*
DFDS A/S, Copenhagen
PoR: Esbjerg

Ex *Scandinavia Star*
Ex *Tor Britannia*

Builders: Flender Werft AG,
Lübeck
Yard no: 607
14,905 GRT; 3,335 DWT; 182.4 ×
23.6 m / 598 × 77.4 ft; Four 12-
cyl geared diesels, Pielstick-
Lindholmens Varv; Twin screw;
34,000 kW (45,600 BHP); 26 kn;
Passengers: 756, plus 512
unberthed, 500 when cruising;
Crew: 143; Private cars: 420.

1974 Oct 10: Launched for Tor
Line A/B, Gothenburg.
1975 May 15: Delivered. 15,657
GRT.
Gothenburg-Felixstowe service.
1976 Gothenburg-Immingham
service.
1978 To S.C. Salén PR,
Stockholm.
1981 Owners recorded as
Saléninvest A/B, Salénia A/B and
Rederi A/B Transatlantic,
Gothenburg.
Nov: Sold to Scandinavian
Seaways (Bahamas) Ltd, Nassau,
subsidiary of DFDS A/S,
Copenhagen. Renamed
Scandinavia Star. Plan for use as
cruiseship not implemented.
1982 Taken over as *Tor Britannia*
of DFDS A/S. 15,794 GRT.
1984 14,905 GRT.

Motorship *Tor Scandinavia*
A/S Difko XXIII, Copenhagen
PoR: Esbjerg

Ex *World Wide Expo*
Ex *Tor Scandinavia*
Ex *Holland Expo*
Ex *Tor Scandinavia*

Builders: Flender Werft AG,
Lübeck
Yard no: 608
14,893 GRT; 3,335 DWT; 182.4 ×
23.6 m / 598 × 77.4 ft; Four 12-
cyl geared diesels, Pielstick-
Lindholmens Varv; Twin screw;
34,000 kW (45,600 BHP); 26 kn;
Passengers: 756, plus 512
unberthed, 500 when cruising;
Crew: 143; Private cars: 420.

1975 Nov 4: Launched for Tor
Line A/B, Gothenburg.
1976 Apr 12: Delivered.
Gothenburg-Felixstowe service.
1979 Jan: Chartered until
February by a Dutch commercial
group to serve as exhibition ship
under name *Holland Expo*.
Toured Persian Gulf.
Feb: Again *Tor Scandinavia*.
1981 To Saléninvest A/B, Salénia
A/B and Rederi A/B
Transatlantic, Gothenburg.
Dec 1: To DFDS A/S, Esbjerg.
1982 Nov: Sailed for Far East as
exhibition ship *World Wide Expo*
in connection with Expo Offshore
Asia 83.
1983 Feb: Again *Tor Scandinavia*.
Nov 17: Sold to A/S Difko XXIII,
Copenhagen. Chartered to DFDS
A/S for 15 years.
1984 14,893 GRT.
1986/87 Again to be exhibition
ship *World Wide Expo*.

1 Tor Britannia *in DFDS colours.*
(Rudie Kleyn.)
2 Tor Scandinavia *in her original
colours.* (Gerhard Fiebiger.)

Motorship *Robin Hood*
Partenreederi ms 'Peter Pan'
PoR: Lübeck

Ex *Peter Pan*

Builders: Werft Nobiskrug
GmbH, Rendsburg
Yard no: 681
12,527 GRT; 2,700 DWT; 148.9 ×
24.0 m / 489 × 78.7 ft; Two 16-
cyl geared diesels, Pielstick-Blohm
+ Voss; Twin screw; 15,500 kW
(20,800 BHP); 22 kn; Passengers:
712, plus 888 unberthed; Crew:
125; Private cars: 470.

1974 Feb 2: Launched for
Travemünde-Trelleborg-Linie
(TT-Linie) GmbH & Co,
Hamburg.
May 22: Delivered.
Maiden cruise Travemünde-
Gothenburg-Oslo.
May 25: Maiden voyage
Travemünde-Trelleborg.
Cruising during winter of her first
year.
1981 Jan: Jointly operated with
Saga-Linjen under designation
TT-Saga-Line.
1984 12,519 GRT.
1985 12,527 GRT. Registered
under ownership of Partenreederi
ms 'Peter Pan'.
1986 Renamed *Robin Hood*.
Reported sold to Minoan Lines,
Iraklion.

Motorship *Abel Tasman*
Government of State of Tasmania
(Transport Commission), Hobart
PoR: Devonport

Ex *Nils Holgersson*

Builders: Werft Nobiskrug
GmbH, Rendsburg
Yard no: 682
12,515 GRT; 2,700 DWT; 148.9 ×
24.0 m / 489 × 78.7 ft; Two 16-
cyl geared diesels, Pielstick-Blohm
+ Voss; Twin screw; 15,500 kW
(20,800 BHP); 22 kn; Passengers:
712, plus 888 unberthed; Crew:
125; Private cars: 470.

1974 Oct 28: Launched as *Nils
Holgersson* for Travemünde-
Trelleborg Linie (TT-Linie)
GmbH & Co, Hamburg.
1975 Apr 8: Delivered. Following
maiden cruise Travemünde-
Gothenburg-Oslo, Travemünde-
Trelleborg service. Cruising during
winter of ship's first year.
1981 Jan: Jointly operated with
Saga-Linjen under designation
TT-Saga-Line.
1984 Sep 20: To subsidiary of
Australian National Line:
Government of State of Tasmania
(Transport Commission), Hobart.
To Nobiskrugwerft GmbH,
Rendsburg, for refit.
1985 Renamed *Abel Tasman*.
Apr 22: Sailed from shipyard on
delivery voyage to Australia.
Apr 23: Strike by stewards forced
abandonment of voyage at
Brunsbüttel. Ship proceeded
through Kiel Canal and laid up at
Kiel from April 26.
May 18: Sailed for Devonport,
Tasmania.

1 *In 1981* Peter Pan *and her sister ship
were given new funnel colours.*
(Achim Borchert.)
2 *The former* Nils Holgersson *is now
the* Abel Tasman. (Gerhard Fiebiger.)

Turbine steamer *Veracruz Primero*
Bahama Cruise Line Inc, New
York/NY
PoR: Panama

Ex *Freeport*
Ex *Carnivale*
Ex *Theodor Herzl*

Builders: Deutsche Werft AG,
Hamburg
Yard no: 697
9,914 GRT; 2,960 DWT; 148.7 ×
18.4 m / 488 × 60.36 ft; Two sets
geared turbines, Allgemeine
Electricitäts Gesellschaft; Twin
screw; 9,430 kW (12,640 SHP); 20
kn; Passengers: 730.

1956 Oct 1: Launched as *Theodor
Herzl*. 9,914 GRT.
1957 Apr 29: Delivered to Zim
Israel Navigation Co Ltd, Haifa.
Passengers: 120 1st class, 450
tourist class.
Haifa-Marseilles service.
1969 Nov: Sold to New Horizons
Shipping Ltd, Chesnut Hill, Mass.
Renamed *Carnivale*. Liberian flag.
Laid up at Toulon.
1971 May 12: Arrived at La
Spezia. Laid up.
1975 Refitted for cruising.
Renamed *Freeport*.
1976 On United States cruising
market. Renamed *Veracruz I*.
1978 To Freeport Cruise Lines,
Panama. 10,596 GRT.
1980 May 26: First voyage New
York-Montreal under charter to
Strand Holidays Ltd.
1981 To Marpan Two Inc,
Panama. Gross tonnage reduced
to original figure of 9,914.
Cruising in Caribbean.
1984 Registered in Panama under
ownership of Common Bros plc,
Newcastle-upon-Tyne (Bahama
Cruise Line Inc, New York).

Motorship *Cunard Countess*
Cunard Cruise Ships Ltd (Cunard
Line Ltd, New York/NY)
PoR: Southampton

Builders: Burmeister & Wain's
Skibsbyggeri A/S, Copenhagen
Yard no: 858
17,593 GRT; 3,230 DWT; 163.6 ×
22.8 m / 537 × 74.8 ft; Four 7-cyl
geared diesels, Burmeister &
Wain-Hitachi; Twin screw; 15,670
kW (21,000 BHP); 21.5 kn;
Passengers: 950.

1974 Sep 20: Launched.
1975 May 21: Delivered.
May 28: Arrived at La Spezia for
internal fitting by Industrie Navali
Mechaniche Affini.
1976 Jul: Completed. 17,495
GRT.
Aug 14: First cruise from San
Juan, Puerto Rico.
1982 Oct: Chartered by British
Government for service
Ascension-Port Stanley, Falkland
Islands.
1983 May: Malta Dry Dock Co
received contract for reconversion
of *Cunard Countess* from
troopship to cruise liner. 17,593
GRT.
Jul: Returned to United States
cruising market.

1 *Contrary to Lloyd's Register,
wherein she is recorded as the*
Veracruz Primero, *this photograph,
taken during her refitting, shows the
name of the ship with a Roman figure
'I' rather than 'Primero'.* (Gerhard
Fiebiger.)
2 *Following her service as a troopship,
the* Cunard Countess *has returned to
cruising.* (J.F. Van Puyvelde.)

Motorship *Cunard Princess*
Cunard Cruise Ships Ltd (Cunard Line Ltd, New York/NY)
PoR: Nassau

Ex *Cunard Conquest*

Builders: Burmeister & Wain's Skibsbyggeri A/S, Copenhagen
Yard no: 859
17,496 GRT; 2,499 DWT; 163.6 × 22.8 m / 537 × 74.8 ft; Four 7-cyl geared diesels, Burmeister & Wain; Twin screw; 15,670 kW (21,000 BHP); 21.25 kn; Passengers: 947.

1974 Dec: Launched as *Cunard Conquest*.
1975 Oct 30: Delivered.
Nov 6: Arrived at La Spezia for internal fitting by Industrie Navali Mechaniche Affini.
1976 Renamed *Cunard Princess*.
1980 Oct: Registered under flag of Bahamas. United States west coast cruising market.

Motorship *Kronprins Harald*
I/S Jahre Line, Sandefjord
PoR: Sandefjord

Builders: Werft Nobiskrug GmbH, Rendsburg
Yard no: 685
13,141 GRT; 2,999 DWT; 156.4 × 23.5 m / 513 × 77.1 ft; Two 20-cyl geared diesels, Stork-Werkspoor; Twin screw; 17,900 kW (24,000 BHP); 22 kn; Passengers: 585 1st class, 415 tourist class; Crew: 138; Private cars: 404.

1975 Oct 4: Launched.
1976 Mar 30: Delivered. 12,752 GRT.
Apr 2: Maiden voyage Oslo-Kiel.
1985 13,141 GRT.
1986 Sep: Reported sold to DFDS A/S Copenhagen.

1 *The* Cunard Princess *represents Cunard in the Caribbean.* (Cunard.)
2 *The* Kronprins Harald *operates between Kiel and Oslo.* (Martin Lochte-Holtgreven.)

Motorship *Napoléon*
Soc Nationale Maritime Corse Méditerranée (SNCM), Marseilles
PoR: Marseilles

Builders: Dubigeon-Normandie SA, Nantes
Yard no: 146
14,918 GRT; 3,000 DWT; 155.0 × 24.0 m / 508 × 78.7 ft; Two 18-cyl geared diesels, Pielstick-Chantiers de l'Atlantique; Twin screw; 25,500 kW (34,200 BHP); 23.5 kn; Passengers: 618 1st class, 830 2nd class; Private cars: 684.

1975 Nov 4: Launched for Cie Générale Transméditerranéenne, reorganised March 1976 as Soc Nationale Maritime Corse Méditerranée.
1976 Jun 21: Maiden voyage Marseilles-Ajaccio-Toulon.

3 *The* Napoléon *is the largest French ferry.* (Antonio Scrimali.)

1

2

3

Gas turbine/diesel-electric vessel
Finnjet
Finnjet Lines Ltd, Helsinki
PoR: Helsinki

Builders: O/Y Wärtsilä A/B,
Helsinki
Yard no: 407
25,042 GRT; 1,885 DWT; 212.8 ×
24.4 m / 698 × 80.1 ft; Two Pratt
& Whitney gas turbines, 56,250
kW (75,000 SHP); also two 18-cyl
diesels, O/Y Wärtsilä, 11,400 kW
(15,500 BHP), coupled to two
Strömberg generators supplying
power to two Strömberg electric
propulsion motors, 14,400 kW
(18,500 BHP), connected to
existing reduction gearing; Twin
screw; 30.5 kn; Passengers: 1,532;
Private cars: 220; Commercial
vehicles: 30.

1976 Mar 28: Floated out of
building dock.
Dec 9: First trials.
Apr: Delivered to Enso-Gutzeit
O/Y (O/Y Finnlines Ltd). 24,605
GRT. 56,000 kW. Gas turbines.
Helsinki-Travemünde service.
1981 Oct: Because of high fuel
consumption by gas turbine
propulsion unit, rebuilt at
Amsterdam to include
supplementary diesel-electric
installation as above.
Dec 13: Returned to service.
25,042 GRT. Using only diesel-
electric propulsion unit vessel can
operate during lightly-trafficked
winter months at speed of 18.5
knots. Speed of 30.5 knots noted
above attained with gas turbines.
1983 Jan 1: Transferred to
ownership of Finnjet Lines Ltd.
1986 Nov: Reported transferred to
Silja group.

Motorship *Sir Robert Bond*
CN Marine Inc, Halifax/NS
PoR: Ottawa

Builders: Port Weller Dry Docks
Ltd, St Catherines, Ontario
Yard no: 59
10,433 GRT; 3,726 DWT; 135.3 ×
21.7 m / 444 × 71 ft; Four 12-cyl
geared diesels, Ruston-Paxman;
Twin screw; 6,743 kW (8,800
BHP); 17 kn; Passengers: 235;
Private cars: 75; Commercial
vehicles: 26.

1975 Launched for Canadian
National Railway Co, Montreal,
PQ.
Following completion, ferry
service in Canadian coastal waters.
1976 Taken over by Department of
Transport, Government of
Canada, Ottawa.
1979 Transferred to CN Marine
Inc, Halifax, NS.

1 *The fastest ferry in the world, the*
Finnjet. (Peter Voss.)
2 *The Canadian ferry* Sir Robert
Bond. (CN Marine.)

1

2

Motorship *Habib*
Cie Tunisienne de Navigation SA
(COTUNAV), Tunis
PoR: Tunis

Builders: Schiffbau Werft
Nobiskrug GmbH, Rendsburg
Yard no: 690
11,179 GRT; 3,372 DWT; 143.3 ×
23.5 m / 470 × 77.1 ft; Four 8-cyl
diesels, Atlas-MaK Maschinenbau;
Twin screw; 17,900 kW (24,000
BHP); 23 kn; Passengers: 658,
plus 488 unberthed; Crew: 135;
Private cars: 350.
1977 Dec 17: Launched.
1978 May 19: Delivered.
Jun 3: Maiden voyage Tunis-
Marseilles. Sails twice-weekly to
Marseilles and once-weekly to
Genoa.

Motorship *Dana Anglia*
K/S Difko XXI (DFDS A/S),
Holsterbro
PoR: Esbjerg

Builders: Aalborg Vaerft A/S,
Aalborg
Yard no: 210
14,400 GRT; 3,440 DWT; 152.9 ×
23.7 m / 502 × 77.8 ft; Two 18-
cyl geared diesels, Lindholmen
Motor; Twin screw; 15,520 kW
(20,800 BHP); 21 kn; Passengers:
1,249, plus 107 unberthed; Crew:
121; Private cars: 470.

1977 Jun 24: Launched.
May: Completed for DFDS A/S,
Copenhagen.
Esbjerg-Harwich service.
1983 Jan: DFDS sold *Dana
Anglia* to Dansk Investering Fond,
chartering her back for ten years.
1984 Registered under ownership
of K/S Difko XXI, Holsterbro.

Motorship *Cyrnos*
Soc Nationale Maritime Corse
Méditerranée (SNCM), Marseilles
PoR: Marseilles

Builders: Dubigeon-Normandie
SA, Nantes
Yard no: 160
11,819 GRT; 2,400 DWT; 137.7 ×
23.0 m / 452 × 75.5 ft; Four 12-
cyl geared diesels, Pielstick-
Chantiers de l'Atlantique; Twin
screw; 23,280 kW (31,200 BHP);
22 kn; Passengers: 1,332, plus 335
unberthed; Crew: 133; Private
cars: 440.

1978 Nov 14: Launched unnamed.
1979 May 31: Delivered.
Jun 18: Named. Maiden voyage
Marseilles-Ajaccio.

1 *Flagship of the Tunisian fleet, the*
Habib. (Peter Voss.)
2 *Her striking funnel sets the* Dana
Anglia *apart.* (Schiffsfotos Jansen.)
3 *The* Cyrnos *was built for the
Marseilles-Corsica service.* (Dubigeon-
Normandie.)

1

2

3

Motorship *Turella*
SF Line A/B (Viking Line),
Mariehamn
PoR: Mariehamn

Builders: O/Y Wärtsilä A/B, Åbo
Yard no: 1242
10,604 GRT; 3,100 DWT; 136.1 ×
24.2 m / 447 × 79.4 ft; Four 12-
cyl geared diesels, Pielstick-O/Y
Wärtsilä; Twin screw; 17,900 kW
(24,000 BHP); 21.5 kn;
Passengers: 750, plus 950
unberthed; Crew: 140; Private
cars: 555.

1978 Nov 24: Launched.
1979 Jun: Completed.
Åbo-Stockholm service.

1 *With the device 'E 3' ('Europe Street
3'), the significance of Viking Line
ships as 'floating roadways' is
emphasised. This is the* Turella.
(Weirauch collection.)
2 *The* Rosella *in icy waters. (Weirauch
collection.)*

Motorship *Rosella*
SF Line A/B (Viking Line),
Mariehamn
PoR: Mariehamn

Builders: O/Y Wärtsilä A/B, Åbo
Yard no: 1249
10,757 GRT; 2,300 DWT; 136.1 ×
24.2 m / 447 × 79.4 ft; Four 12-
cyl geared diesels, Pielstick-O/Y
Wärtsilä; Twin screw; 17,900 kW
(24,000 BHP); 21.5 kn; 750
passengers, plus 950 unberthed;
Crew: 140; Private cars: 555.

1979 Aug 14: Launched.
1980 Apr 21: Delivered.
Finland-Sweden ferry service.
1985 10,757 GRT.

3 *In the box-like design of the
Japanese sister ships* New Suzuran
(illustrated) and New Yukari, *the fore
and aft curve of the deckline displays a
sheer seldom met with in modern
shipbuilding practice. (J.F. Van
Puyvelde.)*

Motorship *New Suzuran*
Shin Nipponkai Ferry KK, Osaka
PoR: Otaru

Builders: Koyo Dock Co Ltd,
Mihara
Yard no: 828
14,586 GRT; 6,150 DWT; 191.8 ×
29.4 m / 629 × 96.5 ft; Two 16-
cyl geared diesels,
Maschinenfabrik Augsburg-
Nürnberg-Mitsubishi Heavy
Industries; Twin screw; 23,870 kW
(32,000 BHP); 22.5 kn;
Passengers: 870; Crew: 64; Private
cars: 46; Commercial vehicles:
163.

1979 Feb 22: Launched.
May: Completed. 14,624 GRT.
Maiden voyage Tsuruga-Otaru.
1981 16,239 GRT.
1983 14,586 GRT.

1

2

3

Motorship *New Yukari*
Shin Nipponkai Ferry KK, Osaka
PoR: Otaru

Builders: Koyo Dock Co Ltd,
Mihara
Yard no: 830
14,582 GRT; 6,161 DWT; 191.8 ×
29.4 m / 629 × 96.5 ft; Two 16-
cyl geared diesels,
Maschinenfabrik Augsburg-
Nürnberg-Mitsubishi Heavy
Industries; Twin screw; 23,870 kW
(32,000 BHP); 22.5 kn;
Passengers: 870; Crew: 64; Private
cars: 46; Commercial vehicles:
163.

1979 Mar 30: Launched.
Jul: Completed. 14,618 GRT.
Tsuruga-Otaru service.
1981 16,250 GRT.
1983 14,582 GRT.

Motorship *Diana II*
P/R Diana II, Carl Bertil Myrsten
(Viking Line), Stockholm
PoR: Site

Builders: Jos. L. Meyer GmbH &
Co, Papenburg
Yard no: 592
11,537 GRT; 2,400 DWT; 137.0 ×
24.2 m / 449 × 79.4 ft; Four 8-cyl
geared diesels, Maschinenfabrik
Augsburg-Nürnberg; Twin screw;
17,900 kW (24,000 BHP); 21 kn;
Passengers: 714, plus 986
unberthed; Crew: 100; Private
cars: 555.

1979 Mar 31: Launched.
Jun 9: Delivered. Registered under
name of *Diana II af Slite*. 11,671
GRT.
Jun 16: Maiden voyage
Stockholm-Mariehamn-Turku.
1984 11,537 GRT.

1 *The* New Yukari. *With a hull
designed for high speed, this
photograph shows her sharp form on
the waterline, where a special recess
has been built in for the bow-wave.*
(J.F. Van Puyvelde.)
2 Diana II *was the first 'jumbo-ferry'
from the yard of Jos. L. Meyer.*
(Arnold Kludas.)

Motorship *Pearl of Scandinavia*
Loke Shipping (Bahamas) Ltd,
Nassau
PoR: Nassau

Ex *Innstar*
Ex *Finnstar*
Ex *Finlandia*

Builders: O/Y Wärtsilä A/B,
Helsinki
Yard no: 383
12,456 GRT; 5,597 DWT; 153.0 ×
20.0 m / 502 × 65.6 ft; Two 9-cyl
geared diesels, Sulzer Bros-O/Y
Wärtsilä; Twin screw; 12,230 kW
(16,400 BHP); 22 kn; Passengers:
437; Crew: 217.

1966 Aug 25: Launched as
Finlandia for Finska Angfartygs
A/B, Helsinki.
1967 May 18: Delivered. 8,168
GRT. Passengers: 270 1st class,
194 2nd class, 200 tourist class.
Private cars: 320.
May 25: Maiden voyage Helsinki-
Copenhagen-Travemünde.
1977 To Enso-Gutzeit O/Y,
Helsinki.
1978 Reconstructed as cruise-ship.
10,311 GRT. Passengers: 576.
Renamed *Finnstar*.

1979 Jan: First cruise Helsinki-
Copenhagen-Bremerhaven-North
Africa.
1980 Aug: Laid up as result of
strike and 17 per cent wage
increase.
1981 Sold to DFDS A/S and I.M.
Skaugen & Co, Oslo, associates
Loke Shipping (Bahamas) Ltd,
Nassau. Renamed *Innstar*.
Aug 18: Arrived at Aalborg where
converted for cruising in Far East
waters. Passengers: 509.
1982 Apr: Conversion completed.
Renamed *Pearl of Scandinavia*.
12,456 GRT.
Jun: Cruising from Hong Kong/
Singapore.
1984 Passengers: 437.

Motorship *Georg Ots*
USSR-Estonian Shipping Co,
Tallin
PoR: Tallin

Builders: Stocznia Szczecinska im
A. Warskiego, Szczecin
Yard no: B493/01
11,496 GRT; 1,363 DWT; 125.0 ×
21.0 m / 410 × 68.9 ft; Four 6-cyl

geared diesels, Zgoda-Sulzer;
Twin screw; 12,800 kW (17,400
BHP); 19 kn; Passengers: 216,
plus 784 unberthed; Crew: 186.

1979 Nov: Launched.
1980 Delivered, then Tallin-
Leningrad-Helsinki service.

Motorship *White Sanpo 2*
Sanpo Kaiun KK, Imabari
PoR: Imbari

Builders: Hayashikane
Shipbuilding & Engineering Co
Ltd, Shimonoseki
Yard no: 1240
10,181 GRT; 3,725 DWT; 155.8 ×
23.6 m / 510 × 77.4 ft; Two 18-
cyl geared diesels, Pielstick-
Nippon Kokan KK; Twin screw;
17,460 kW (23,400 BHP); 21 kn;
Passengers: 1,050.

1981 Feb: Launched.
Jun: Entered service as passenger
and car ferry.

1 *In 1978 the ferry* Finlandia *became
the cruise-ship* Finnstar. *She now
serves in the Far East as the* Pearl of
Scandinavia. *(Arnold Kludas.)*

1

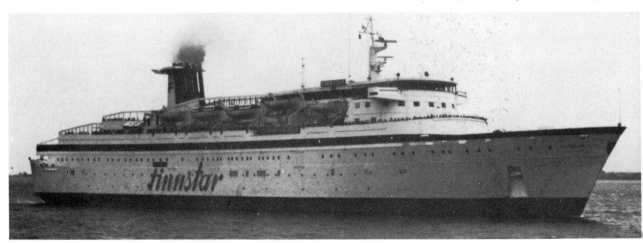

2

2 *The* George Ots *was built for ferry service in the Baltic.* (Peter Voss.)

3 *A most distinctive colour scheme identifies the* White Sanpo 2. (Y. Yokoi.)

3

Motorship *Liberté*
Soc Nationale Maritime Corse
Méditerranée (SNCM), Marseilles
PoR: Marseilles

Builders: Dubigeon-Normandie
SA, Nantes
Yard no: 161
10,766 GRT; 1,700 DWT; 141.5 ×
21.9 m / 464 × 71.9 ft; Two 18-
cyl geared diesels, Pielstick-
Chantiers de l'Atlantique; Twin
screw; 17,460 kW (23,400 BHP);
21.5 kn; Passengers: 454 cabin
class, 638 3rd class.

1979 Dec 5: Launched unnamed.
1980 Jun 19: Named.
Jun 22: Delivered.
Marseilles-North Africa service
and mini cruises. 12,000 GRT.
1984 10,766 GRT.

1 *None of the Dubigeon ferries is
exactly alike. The* Liberté *is fitted in
addition for mini cruising.* (Dubigeon
Normandie.)
2 *The* Peter Wessel, *ex* Wasa Star.
(Achim Borchert.)
3 *The largest ship of A/B Gotland, the*
Visby. (Øresundsvarvet.)

Motorship *Peter Wessel*
A/S Larvik-Frederikshavnferjen,
Larvik
PoR: Larvik

Ex *Wasa Star*

Builders: Øresundsvarvet A/B,
Landskrona
Yard no: 279
14,919 GRT; 2,410 DWT; 142.3 ×
24.0 m / 467 × 78.7 ft; Four 8-cyl
geared diesels, Burmeister &
Wain-Götaverken; Twin screw;
21,470 kW (28,790 BHP); 21 kn;
Passengers: 1,100, plus 850
unberthed; Private cars: 515.

1980 Dec 5: Floated out of
building dock.
1981 Jun 24: Delivered.
Because of their size the *Wasa Star*
and her sister ship *Visby* could be
handled only with difficulty in
their intended terminal port of
Visby. Pending completion of
projected improvements to Visby
harbour *Wasa Star* was laid up.
Currently being operated on

Mediterranean charter between
Ancona and Patras.
1984 Aug: To A/S Larvik-
Frederikshavnferjen, Larvik.
Renamed *Peter Wessel*.

Motorship *Visby*
Rederi A/B Gotland, Visby
PoR: Visby

Builders: Øresundsvarvet A/B
Landskrona
Yard no: 278
15,001 GRT; 2,840 DWT; 142.3 ×
24.0 m / 467 × 78.7 ft; Two 8-cyl
geared diesels, Burmeister &
Wain-Götaverken; Twin screw;
21,780 kW (29,200 BHP); 21 kn;
Passengers: 1,142, plus 858
unberthed; Private cars: 515.

1980 Jan 25: Floated out of
building dock. Intended name
Farja.
Oct 10: Delivered. 14,932 GRT.
Visby-Neynäsham service.
1984 15,001 GRT.

1

2

3

Motorship *Dronning Ingrid*
Government of the Kingdom of
Denmark (Danske Statsbaner),
Copenhagen
PoR: Korsör

Builders: Helsingör Vaerft A/S,
Elsinore
Yard no: 418
10,607 GRT; 4,150 DWT; 148.1 ×
22.8 m / 486 × 74.8 ft; Six 16-cyl
geared diesels, Burmeister &
Wain-Alpha Diesel; Twin screw;
18,950 kW (25,400 BHP); 19 kn;
Passengers: 2,000 unberthed; Rail
track: 490 m.

1980 Jan 25: Launched.
Jun: Delivered.
Train ferry service Nyborg-
Korsör.

Motorship *Kronprins Frederik*
Government of the Kingdom of
Denmark (Danske Statsbaner),
Copenhagen
PoR: Korsör

Builders: A/S Nakskov
Skibsvaerft, Nakskov
Yard no: 224
10,606 GRT; 4,277 DWT; 152.0 ×
22.8 m / 499 × 74.8 ft; Six 16-cyl
geared diesels, Burmeister &
Wain-Alpha Diesel; Twin screw;
17,200 kW (23,000 BHP); 19 kn;
Passengers: 2,000 unberthed; Rail
track: 490 m.

1980 Jul 2: Launched.
1981 Apr 2: Delivered.
Train ferry service Nyborg-
Korsör.

1 *The first train ferry to exceed 10,000
GRT, the* Dronning Ingrid *came into
service in 1980.* (Achim Borchert.)
2 *The* Kronprins Frederik *during
trials.* (A/S Nakskov.)

Motorship *Prins Joachim*
Government of the Kingdom of
Denmark (Danske Statsbaner),
Copenhagen
PoR: Korsör

Builders: A/S Nakskov
Skibsvaerft, Nakskov
Yard no: 223
10,607 GRT; 4,490 DWT; 152.0 ×
22.8 m / 499 × 74.8 ft; Six 16-cyl
geared diesels, Burmeister &
Wain-Alpha Diesel; Twin screw;
17,200 kW (23,000 BHP); 19 kn;
Passengers: 2,000 unberthed; Rail
track: 490 m.

1980 Jan 25: Launched.
Jul 2: Delivered.
Train ferry service Nyborg-
Korsör.

Motorship *Viking Saga*
Suomen Yritysrahoitus O/Y,
Helsinki
PoR: Mariehamn

Builders: O/Y Wärtsilä A/B, Åbo
Yard no: 1247
14,330 GRT; 2,874 DWT; 145.2 ×
25.2 m / 476 × 82.7 ft; Four 12-
cyl geared diesels, Pielstick-O/Y
Wärtsilä; Twin screw; 19,400 kW
(26,000 BHP); 21.3 kn;
Passengers: 1,104, plus 896
unberthed; Private cars: 540;
Commercial vehicles: 60.

1980 Jan 4: Launched for Rederi
A/B Sally, Mariehamn.
Jul 21: Delivered.
Stockholm-Helsinki service.
1982 Sold to Finska Angfartygs
A/B (EFFOA), Helsinki.
Management by Rederi A/B Sally,
Mariehamn.
1984 Sold to Yritysrahoitus O/Y,
Helsinki.

Motorship *Braemar*
Partrederi Braemar (Fred Olsen &
Co), Oslo
PoR: Kristiansand

Ex Viking Song

Builders: O/Y Wärtsilä A/B, Åbo
Yard no: 1248
14,623 GRT; 2,830 DWT; 145.2 ×
25.2 m / 476 × 82.7 ft; Four 12-
cyl geared diesels, Pielstick-O/Y
Wärtsilä; Twin screw; 19,400 kW
(26,000 BHP); Passengers: 1,104,
plus 896 unberthed; Private cars:
540; Commercial vehicles: 60.

1980 Feb 15: Launched as *Viking
Song* for Rederi A/B Sally,
Mariehamn.
Aug 29: Delivered.
Stockholm-Mariehamn-Helsinki
service.
1985 Feb: Sold to Fred Olsen &
Co, Oslo.
May 15: Arrived at Hamburg for
refitting by Blohm + Voss AG.
14,623 GRT.
June 6: Sailed from Hamburg for
Kristiansand where renamed
Braemar.
Kristiansand-Harwich, from
September Oslo-Hirtshals-
Harwich service.

1 *The last of three sister ships to come into service, the* Prins Joachim. (Achim Borchert.)

1

2 *The Wärtsilä yard at Åbo built the sister ships* Viking Saga *(illustrated) and* Viking Song *for the Viking Line shipping group.* (Schiffsfotos Jansen.)

2

3 *The* Braemar *in June 1985, showing a new Olsen guise.* (Peter Voss.)

3

Motorship *Viking Sally*
Rederi A/B Sally, Mariehamn
PoR: Mariehamn

Builders: Jos. L. Meyer GmbH &
Co, Papenburg
Yard no: 590
15,566 GRT; 3,345 DWT; 155.4 ×
24.2 m / 510 × 79.4 ft; Four 8-cyl
geared diesels, Maschinenfabrik
Augsburg-Nürnberg; Twin screw;
17,900 kW (24,000 BHP); 21.2 kn;
Passengers: 828, plus 358
unberthed; Crew: 110; Private
cars: 460.

1980 Apr 26: Launched.
Jun 29: Delivered.
Åbo-Mariehamn-Stockholm
service.

Motorship *Silvia Regina*
Suomen Yritysrahoitus O/Y,
Helsinki
PoR: Mariehamn

Builders: O/Y Wärtsilä A/B, Åbo
Yard no: 1252
25,905 GRT; 3,898 DWT; 166.1 ×
28.4 m / 545 × 93.2 ft; Four 12-
cyl geared diesels, Pielstick-O/Y
Wärtsilä; Twin screw; 22,950 kW
(31,200 BHP); 22 kn; Passengers:
1,621, plus 379 unberthed; Crew:
164; Private cars: 480.

1980 Oct 21: Launched for O/Y
Svea Line (Finland) A/B,
Helsinki, subsidiary of
Stockholms Rederi A/B Svea,
Stockholm. Intended name *Silja
Star*. Following acquisition in 1981
of Rederi A/B Svea by Johnson
Line A/B, Stockholm, ship
acquired by Finnish Corporate
Finance Ltd, Helsinki.
1981 Jun 10: Delivered as *Silvia
Regina*.
In Silja Line service Helsinki-
Stockholm, operated by Finska
Angfartygs A/B (EFFOA),
Helsinki.
1984 Sold to Suomen
Yritysrahoitus O/Y, Helsinki.
Managers: Finska Angfartygs A/B
(EFFOA).

1 *The* Viking Sally *continues the trend
towards increasingly large ferries for
Baltic service.* (Schiffsfotos Jansen.)
2 *The* Silvia Regina *surpasses in size
her sister ship* Finlandia. (Weirauch
collection.)

1

2

Motorship *Finlandia*
Finska Angfartygs A/B (EFFOA),
Helsinki
PoR: Helsinki

Builders: O/Y Wärtsilä A/B, Åbo
Yard no: 1251
25,905 GRT; 3,898 DWT; 166.1 ×
28.4 m / 545 × 93.2 ft; Four 12-
cyl geared diesels, Pielstick-O/Y
Wärtsilä; Twin screw; 22,950 kW
(31,200 BHP); 20, max 22 kn;
Passengers: 1,594, plus 416
unberthed; Crew: 164; Private
cars: 480.

1980 Jul 25: Launched. Intended
name *Skandia*.
1981 Mar 30: Delivered as
Finlandia.
Helsinki-Stockholm service of
Silja Line. 25,678 GRT.
1984 25,905 GRT.

Motorship *Prinsesse Ragnhild*
I/S Jahre Line, Oslo
PoR: Sandefjord

Builders: Howaldtswerke-
Deutsche Werft AG, Kiel
Yard no: 164
16,608 GRT; 3,210 DWT; 170.0 ×
24.0 m / 558 × 78.7 ft; Two 20-
cyl geared diesels, Stork-
Werkspoor; Twin screw; 17,660
kW (23,700 BHP); 21.75 kn;
Passengers: 896; Crew: 112;
Private cars: 603.

1980 Aug 1: Floated out of
building dock.
1981 Jan 31: Named and
delivered. 16,331 GRT.
Oslo-Kiel service.
1984 16,608 GRT.

Motorship *Esterel*
Soc Nationale Maritime Corse
Méditerranée (SNCM), Marseilles
PoR: Marseilles

Builders: Dubigeon-Normandie
SA, Nantes
Yard no: 162
12,676 GRT; 2,200 DWT; 145.0 ×
23.8 m / 476 × 78.1 ft; Four 16-
cyl geared diesels, Pielstick-
Chantiers de l'Atlantique; Twin
screws; 20,550 kW (27,550 BHP);
23.5 kn; Passengers: 572 in two
classes; Crew: 123; Private cars:
700.

1980 Sep 26: Launched unnamed.
1981 May 15: Named and
delivered.
Marseilles-Corsica service.

1 *The* Finlandia *displaced the* Finnjet
as the world's largest ferry.
(Schiffsfotos Jansen.)
2 *The* Princess Ragnhild, *Norway's
largest ferry.* (Peter Voss.)

3 *The* Esterel, *another in the sequence
of deliveries from the Dubigeon
Normandie yard towards the modernisation of France's Mediterranean
ferry fleet.* (Dubigeon Normandie.)

1

2

3

Motorship *Kronprinsessan Victoria*
R/A Göteborg-Frederikshavn Linjen, Gothenburg
PoR: Gothenburg

Builders: Goteverken Arendal A/B, Gothenburg
Yard no: 908
14,378 GRT; 3,315 DWT; 149.1 × 26.0 m / 489 × 85.3 ft; Four 12-cyl geared diesels, O/Y Wärtsilä; Twin screw; 15,370 kW (20,600 BHP); 21 kn; Passengers: 1,734; Private cars: 500.

1980 Oct 15: Launched for Sessan Linjen, Gothenburg.
1981 Mar 1: Trials. Stena Line, Gothenburg, acquired 48 per cent share in Sessan Linjen.
Apr 10: Delivered to Sessan-Stena-founded R/A Göteborg-Frederikshavn Linjen, Gothenburg.
Apr 13: Maiden voyage Gothenburg-Frederikshavn. Passengers on this route: 616, plus 1,484 unberthed. Private cars: 600.
1982 First voyage Gothenburg-Kiel, for which refitted at Gothenburg. Passengers: 1,734. Private cars: 500.

Motorship *St Nicholas*
Hill Samuel Trading (No 26) Ltd (Stena Ferry A/B), Gothenburg
PoR: London

Ex *Prinsessan Birgitta*
Ex *Drottning Silvia*

Builders: Gotaverken Arendal A/B, Gothenburg
Yard no: 909
14,368 GRT; 3,315 DWT; 149.1 × 26.0 m / 489 × 85.3 ft; Four 12-cyl geared diesels, O/Y Wärtsilä; Twin screw; 15,150 kW (20,600 BHP); 21 kn; Passengers: 1,734, plus 400 unberthed; Private cars: 500.

1981 Launched for Sessan Linjen, Gothenburg. Ordered for Frederikshavn-Gothenburg service.
Mar: Stena Line A/B, Gothenburg, acquired 48 per cent share in Sessan Linjen.
1982 Jan: Intended name *Drottning Silvia* not approved by Swedish Royal House. Laid up by builders.
May: Bought by Stena Line who had ship registered under ownership of Stena Sessan Linjen A/B, Gothenburg.
Jun 3: Still unnamed, as yard number 909 made maiden voyage Gothenburg-Frederikshavn.
Jun 7: Named *Prinsessan Birgitta*.
1983 Feb 27: Arrived at Götaverken yard for refit. Former day-service accommodation for 616 passengers, plus 1,484 unberthed, and 600 private cars, altered to 500 1st class and 1,600 2nd class, for Gothenburg-Kiel service.
Jun: Chartered for three years to Sealink UK Ltd. Harwich-Hook of Holland service. Renamed *St*

Nicholas for duration of charter and registered at London in name of Hill Samuel Trading (No 26) Ltd.

1 *With a completely new fashioning, the sister ships* Kronprinsessan Victoria *(illustrated) and* Prinsessan Birgitta *came into service in 1982.* (Martin Lochte-Holtgreven.)
2 *The* St Nicholas, *ex* Prinsessan Birgitta, *sails under the British flag on Sealink service.* (Achim Borchert.)

1

2

Motorship *Tropicale*
Festivale Maritime Inc, Monrovia
PoR: Monrovia

Builders: Aalborg Vaerft A/S,
Aalborg
Yard no: 234
22,919 GRT; 6,654 DWT; 204.8 ×
26.3 m / 672 × 86.3 ft; Two 7-cyl
diesels, Sulzer Bros; Twin screw;
19,566 kW (26,600 BHP); 21 kn;
Passengers: 1,422; Crew: 491.

1980 Oct 31: Launched.
Dec 4: Delivered. Registered under
ownership of AVL Marine Inc,
Monrovia.
Jan: Cruising for Carnival Cruise
Lines Inc on United States market.

1 *There are no limits when it comes to
the introduction of new outlines in
passenger-ship building. The* Tropicale
proves this. (Aalborg Vaerft.)
2 *The* Olau Hollandia, *at the date of
her commissioning, was Germany's
largest ferry. The distinction has now
passed to the new* Peter Pan. (Peter
Voss.)
3 *The* Olau Britannia *followed a year
after her sister. The windows on the
bridge-front are only painted
'dummies'.* (Arnold Kludas.)

Motorship *Olau Hollandia*
Olau Linie (UK) Ltd & Co,
Hamburg
PoR: Hamburg

Builders: AG 'Weser'
Seebeckwerft, Bremerhaven
Yard no: 1028
14,981 GRT; 2,875 DWT; 153.4 ×
24.2 m / 503 × 79.4 ft; Four 8-cyl
geared diesels, Pielstick-Blohm +
Voss; Twin screw; 15,520 kW
(20,800 BHP); 21 kn; Passengers:
938, plus 662 unberthed; Crew:
157; Private cars: 550.

1980 Nov 22: Launched.
1981 Mar 21: Delivered. 15,200
GRT.
1984 14,981 GRT.
Mar 25: Maiden voyage Flushing-
Sheerness service.

Motorship *Olau Britannia*
Olau Linie (UK) Ltd & Co,
Hamburg
PoR: Hamburg

Builders: AG 'Weser'
Seebeckwerft, Bremerhaven
Yard no: 1031
14,983 GRT; 2,880 DWT; 153.4 ×
24.2 m / 503 × 79.4 ft; Four 8-cyl
geared diesels, Pielstick-Blohm +
Voss; Twin screw; 15,520 kW
(20,800 BHP); 21 kn; Passengers:
846, plus 662 unberthed; Crew:
157; Private cars: 550.

1981 Dec 5: Launched.
1982 May 5: Delivered. Originally
for Baltic Sea service of
Travemünde-Trelleborg-Linie
(TT-Linie) GmbH & Co,
Hamburg, but this company,
parent company of Olau Linie
(UK) Ltd & Co, transferred her to
English Channel service.
May 7: Formal naming ceremony
at Sheerness.
Flushing-Sheerness service.
1984 Aug 25: Collided off the
Schelde Estuary with French ro-ro
ship *Mont Louis,* which sank.

1

2

3

Motorship *Arkona*
VEB Deutfracht/Seereederei,
Rostock
PoR: Rostock

Ex *Astor*

Builders: Howaldtswerke-
Deutsche Werft AG, Hamburg
Yard no: 165
18,835 GRT; 2,500 DWT; 164.3 ×
22.6 m / 539 × 74.1 ft; Four 6-cyl
geared diesels, Maschinenfabrik
Augsburg-Nürnberg; Twin screw;
9,700 kW (13,200 BHP); 18 kn;
Passengers: 638; Crew: 220.

1980 Dec 16: Launched as *Astor*
for Hadag Seetouristik &
Fahrdienst AG, Hamburg.
Intended name *Hammonia*.
1981 May 21: Comparatively small
fire caused so much smoke and
water damage that maiden voyage
planned to start August 22 had to
be cancelled.
Nov 24: First trials.
Dec 4: Delivered.
Dec 14: Shakedown cruise,
Hamburg-Le Havre-Malaga-
Genoa.
Dec 23: Maiden voyage, Genoa-
North Africa-Tenerife cruise. In
American waters during winter.
1983 Oct 14: Sold to South
African Marine Corp Ltd, Cape
Town.
1984 Feb 7: Delivered. Durban-
Port Elizabeth-Cape Town-Las
Palmas-Southampton service.
Cruising.
1985 Jul 1: Bahamian flag.
Registered at Nassau.
Aug 29: Delivered to VEB
Deutfracht/Seereederei, Rostock.
Renamed *Arkona*.
Oct 25: First cruise Rostock-
Leningrad-Riga.

During summer employed on West
German market.

Motorship *Europa*
Hapag-Lloyd AG, Hamburg
PoR: Bremen

Builders: Bremer Vulkan,
Schiffbau & Maschinenfabrik,
Vegesack
Yard no: 1001
33,819 GRT; 6,506 DWT; 199.6 ×
28.5 m / 655 × 93.5 ft; Two 7-cyl
geared diesels, Maschinenfabrik
Augsburg-Nürnberg-Bremer
Vulkan; Twin screw; 21,270 kW
(28,920 BHP); 21 kn; Passengers:
758; Crew: 300.

1980 Dec 22: Launched.
1981 Sep 25: First trials.
Dec 5: Delivered. Registered under
ownership of Bremer
Schiffsvercharterungs AG & Co
KG.
Dec 28: Positioning voyage
without passengers, Bremerhaven-
Genoa.
1982 Jan 8: Maiden voyage,
Genoa-North Africa cruise. Then
worldwide cruising.

1 *The* Arkona, *ex* Astor. *In four year*
she sailed under as many flags. (Pete
Voss.)
2 *The new* Europa *of Hapag-Lloyd*
AG is one of the world's few real
luxury liners. (Peter Voss.)

Motorship *Atlantic*
Home Lines Inc (Soc de Gestion
Evge SA, Piraeus)
PoR: Monrovia

Builders: Constructions Navales &
Industrielles de la Méditerranée,
La Seyne
Yard no: 1432
19,337 GRT; 7,000 DWT; 204.7 ×
27.4 m / 672 × 90.0 ft; Two 10-
cyl diesels, FIAT-OM
Applicazioni Industriali; Twin
screw; 22,070 kW (30,000 BHP);
23 kn; Passengers: 1,179; Crew:
447.

1981 Jan 9: Launched.
1982 Apr 2: Delivered to Home
Lines Inc, Monrovia.
Apr 14: Arrived at New York for
first time.
Apr 17: Maiden voyage New
York-Bermudas. Mainly cruising
in United States waters.
1985 Registered under ownership
of Home Lines Inc (Soc de
Gestion Evge SA, Piraeus).

Motorship *Saint Killian II*
Irish Continental Line Ltd, Dublin
PoR: Dublin

Ex *Saint Killian*
Ex *Stena Scandinavica*

Builders: Brodogradliste Titovo,
Kraljevica
Yard no: 400
10,256 GRT; 1,471 DWT; 156.9 ×
19.6 m / 515 × 64.3 ft; Two 18-
cyl diesels, Pielstick-Lindholmen
Motor; Twin screw; 13,430 kW
(18,000 BHP); 21.5 kn;
Passengers: 2,119; Private cars:
378.

1972 Sep: Launched as *Stena
Scandinavica* for Stena A/B,
Gothenburg.
1973 Completed. 6,667 GRT.
Length: 124.8 m (409 ft).
Passengers: 873, plus 727
unberthed. Private cars: 278.
Gothenburg-Kiel-Korsör service.
1978 Sold Irish Continental Line
Ltd, Dublin. Renamed *Saint
Killian*.
May: First voyage Rosslare-
Cherbourg service.
1981 To Amsterdamsche
Droogdok Maats NV,
Amsterdam. Lengthened by
32.1 m (106 ft). Passenger
accommodation and private car
capacity increased. 10,256 GRT.
1982 Feb 26: Delivered following
alterations. 'Showing the flag'
visits to several European ports.
Renamed *Saint Killian II*.
Mar 15: Returned to service,
Rosslare-Le Havre.

1 *Comparing the dimensions of the*
Europe *and the* Atlantic *(illustrated),
the understatement of the tonnage of
the new Home liner becomes obvious.*
(Bill Miller collection.)
2 *Lengthening of the* Saint Killian
*brought her gross tonnage to more
than 10,000.* (Florent Van Otterdijk.)

Motorship *Trelleborg*
Government of the Kingdom of
Sweden, Statens Jarnvagar
Farjedriften, Malmö
PoR: Trelleborg

Builders: Øresundsvarvet A/B,
Landskrona
Yard no: 271
10,882 GRT; 3,800 DWT; 170.2 ×
23.8 m / 558 × 78.1 ft; Four 8-cyl
geared diesels, Maschinenfabrik
Augsburg-Nürnberg; Twin screw;
17,650 kW (24,000 BHP); 17.5 kn;
Passengers: 47, plus 753
unberthed; Crew: 138; Private
cars: 15; Commercial vehicles: 20;
Railway vehicles: 55; Rail track:
700 m.

1981 May 19: Floated out of
building dock.
Dec: Trials. Stability problems
apparent with consequent
insufficient carrying capacity.
Since Øresundsvarvet, because of
their impending closure, no longer
had free space, necessary
alterations were carried out at
Götaverken City Works. The
addition of a 95 m (311 ft) long
'bulge' to each side achieved
desired result.
1982 May 28: Delivered. Train-
ferry service between Trelleborg
and Sassnitz.

Motorship *Stardancer*
Sundance Cruises Corp (*vide* notes
re *Pegasus*, page 110)
PoR: Nassau

Ex *Scandinavia*

Builders:
Dubigeon-Normandie SA, Nantes
Yard no: 164
26,747 GRT; 4,000 DWT; 185.0 ×
27.0 m / 607 × 88.6 ft; Two 9-cyl
diesels, Burmeister & Wain-
Chantiers de l'Atlantique; Twin
screw; 19,800 kW (26,600 BHP);
20 kn; Passengers: 1,606; Crew:
350; Private cars: 530.

1981 Oct 16: Launched as
Scandinavia.
Jul: Completed. Registered under
ownership of The United
Steamships Co (Bahamas) Ltd,
Nassau (DFDS A/S,
Copenhagen).
Oct: Maiden voyage, New York-
Bahamas service of Scandinavian
World Cruises.
1984 Transferred to Europe by
DFDS. Copenhagen-Oslo service.
Nov: Sold to Sundance Cruises
Corp. Delivery April 1985.
1985 Apr 29: Delivered as
Stardancer following refit at
Hamburg by Blohm + Voss AG.
Apr 30: Sailed on positioning
voyage to United States. Cruising.

1 *Sweden's largest train ferry, the*
Trelleborg. *(Øresundsvarvet.)*
2 *The* Stardancer *leaving the River*
Elbe after her conversion. (Peter
Voss.)

Motorship *Song of America*
Royal Caribbean Cruise Line A/S
(I.M. Skaugen & Co), Oslo
PoR: Oslo

Builders: O/Y Wärtsilä A/B,
Helsinki
Yard no: 431
37,584 GRT; 5,237 DWT; 214.4 ×
28.4 m / 703 × 93.2 ft; Four 8-cyl
geared diesels, Sulzer Bros-O/Y
Wärtsilä; Twin screw; 16,480 kW
(22,400 BHP); 21 kn; Passengers:
1,414 (max 1,575); Crew: 500.

1981 Nov 26: Floated out of
building dock.
1982 Nov 9: Delivered.
Dec 5: Maiden voyage, cruise
Miami-West Indies.

Motorship *Abegweit*
CN Marine Inc, Halifax/NS
PoR: Charlottetown

Builders: Saint John Shipbuilding
& Dry Dock Co Ltd, Saint John/
NB
Yard no: 1136
13,483 GRT; 4,500 DWT; 122.4 ×
21.5 m / 402 × 70.5 ft; Six 16-cyl
geared diesels, Ruston Diesels;
Twin screw; 15,000 kW (20,400
BHP); 17 kn; Passengers: 950
unberthed; Private cars: 251;
Trailers: 40; Railway vehicles: 20.

1982 Feb 20: Launched.
Ice-breaking ferry in
Northumberland Strait between
Borden and Cape Tormentine.

1 *At the time of her entry into service
the* Song of America *was the largest
purpose-built cruise-ship.* (Martin
Lochte-Holtgreven.)
2 *The most recent CN Marine ferry,
the* Abegweit. (CN Marine.)

1

2

Motorship *Nieuw Amsterdam*
Holland America Tours, Curaçao
PoR: St Maarten

Builders: Chantiers de
l'Atlantique, St Nazaire
Yard no: V 27
33,930 GRT; 4,217 DWT; 214.7 ×
27.2 m / 704 × 89.2 ft; Two 7-cyl
diesels, Sulzer Bros; Twin screw;
21,600 kW (29,400 BHP); 21 kn;
Passengers: 1,374; Crew: 559.

1982 Aug 20: Launched.
1983 May 11: Planned delivery
postponed since fitting-out not
completed. First planned cruise
accordingly held up.
Jan 24: At Le Havre main
switchboard burned out. Naming
and maiden voyage postponed for
second time. Naming planned for
June 25 and maiden voyage to
New York on June 26. Guests of
honour and passengers already
embarked had to return home.
Jul 10: Maiden voyage Le Havre-
New York. United States cruise
market.

Motorship *Noordam*
Holland America Tours, Curaçao
PoR: St Maarten

Builders: Chantiers de
l'Atlantique, St Nazaire
Yard no: X 27
33,933 GRT; 4,243 DWT; 214.7 ×
27.2 m / 704 × 89.2 ft; Two 7-cyl
diesels, Sulzer; Twin screw; 21,600
kW (29,400 BHP); 21 kn;
Passengers: 1,210; Crew: 560.

1983 May 21: Launched.
1984 Delivered.
Apr 8: Maiden voyage Le Havre-
Tampa. Cruising in US waters.

Motorship *Corse*
Soc Nationale Maritime
Méditerranée (SNCM), Marseilles
PoR: Marseilles

Builders: Dubigeon-Normandie
SA, Nantes
Yard no: 163
12,686 GRT; 2,275 DWT; 145.0 ×
23.8 m / 476 × 78.1 ft; Four 16-
cyl geared diesels, Pielstick-
Chantiers de l'Atlantique; Twin
screw; 20,550 kW (27,550 BHP);
22.5 kn; Passengers: 810 in two
classes, plus 1,516 unberthed;
Crew: 123; Private cars: 700.

1982 Oct 16: Launched.
1983 Delivered by Chantiers
Dubigeon (builders' style since
early in year).
Marseilles-Corsica service.

1 *After early teething troubles the*
Nieuw Amsterdam *has now taken up
her cruise programme. (Holland
America Cruises.)*
2 *Holland America Cruises'* Noordam.
(Weirauch collection.)
3 *The* Corse *shortly before delivery.
(Dubigeon Normandie.)*

1

2

3

Motorship *Kerinci*
Government of the Republic of
Indonesia (Ministry of Transport,
Communications & Tourism),
Jakarta
PoR: Padang

Builders: Jos. L. Meyer GmbH &
Co, Papenburg
Yard no: 608
13,954 GRT; 2,750 DWT; 144.0 ×
23.4 m / 472 × 76.8 ft; Two 6-cyl
geared diesels, MaK
Maschinenbau; Twin screw;
12,500 kW (17,000 BHP); 20 kn;
Passengers: 100 1st class, 200 2nd
class, 300 3rd class, 496 4th class,
500 in dormitories; Crew: 119.

1983 May 7: Launched.
Jul 14: Delivered.
Indonesian inter-island traffic and
pilgrim trade.

Motorship *Kambuna*
Government of the Republic of
Indonesia (Ministry of Transport,
Communications & Tourism),
Jakarta
PoR: Ujung Pandang

Builders: Jos. L. Meyer GmbH &
Co, Papenburg
Yard no: 609
13,944 GRT; 3,434 DWT; 144.0 ×
23.4 m / 472 × 76.8 ft; Two 6-cyl
geared diesels, MaK
Maschinenbau; Twin screw;
10,900 kW (14,800 BHP); 20 kn;
Passengers: 100 1st class, 200 2nd
class, 300 3rd class, 496 4th class,
500 in dormitories; Crew: 119.

1983 Oct 15: Launched.
1984 Feb 18: Delivered.
Indonesian inter-island traffic and
pilgrim trade.

Motorship *Rinjani*
Government of the Republic of
Indonesia (Ministry of Transport,
Communications & Tourism),
Jakarta
PoR: Lembar

Builders: Jos. L. Meyer GmbH &
Co, Papenburg
Yard no: 611
13,860 GRT; 3,434 DWT; 144.0 ×
23.4 m / 472 × 76.8 ft; Two 6-cyl
geared diesels, MaK
Maschinenbau; Twin screw;
10,900 kW (14,800 BHP); 20 kn;
Passengers: 100 1st class, 200 2nd
class, 300 3rd class, 496 4th class,
500 in dormitories; Crew: 119.

1984 Feb 18: Launched.
Sep 15: Delivered.
Indonesian inter-island traffic and
pilgrim trade.

1 The Kerinci *entered service as the
first of four sister ships.* (Jos. L.
Meyer.)
2 *Ready for delivery:* Kambuna *on
February 18, 1984.* (Steffen
Weirauch.)

3 The Rinjani *leaving her builders
yard.* (Steffen Weirauch.)

1

Motorship *Umsini*
Government of the Republic of
Indonesia (Ministry of Transport,
Communications & Tourism),
Jakarta
PoR: Sorong

Builders: Jos. L. Meyer GmbH &
Co, Papenburg
Yard no: 612
13,853 GRT; 3,434 DWT; 144.0 ×
23.4 m / 472 × 76.8 ft; Two 6-cyl
geared diesels, MaK
Maschinenbau; Twin screw;
10,900 kW (14,800 BHP); 20 kn;
Passengers: 100 1st class, 200 2nd
class, 300 3rd class, 496 4th class,
500 in dormitories; Crew: 119.

1984 Sep 15: Launched.
1985 Jan 31: Delivered.
Indonesian inter-island traffic and
pilgrim trade.

Motorship *Stena Danica*
Stena Line A/B, Gothenburg
PoR: Gothenburg

Builders: Chantiers du Nord & de
la Méditerranée, Dunkirk
Yard no: 309
15,899 GRT; 2,950 DWT; 152.2 ×
28.0 m / 499 × 91.9 ft; Four 12-
cyl geared diesels, Cie de
Construction Mécanique-Sulzer;
Twin screw; 26,000 kW (34,800
BHP); 22 kn; Passengers: 96, plus
2,204 unberthed; Crew: 140 max.

1980 Aug 30: Launched.
Because of serious technical
problems with machinery
installation, delivery postponed
more than six months.
1983 Feb 27: Naming ceremony at
Gothenburg. 16,494 GRT.
Gothenburg-Frederikshavn service
(approximate crossing-time three
hours).
1984 15,899 GRT.

Motorship *Stena Jutlandica*
Stena Line A/B, Gothenburg
PoR: Gothenburg

Builders: Chantiers du Nord & de
la Méditerranée, Dunkirk
Yard no: 310
15,811 GRT; 2,950 DWT; 152.2 ×
28.0 m / 499 × 91.9 ft; Four 12-
cyl geared diesels, Cie de
Construction Mécanique-Sulzer;
Twin screw; 26,000 kW (34,800
BHP); 22 kn; Passengers: 96, plus
2,204 unberthed; Crew: 140 max.

1980 Dec 22: Launched. As was
case with sister ship *Stena Danica*,
technical difficulties delayed
delivery by several months.
1983 Apr 24: Naming ceremony at
Gothenburg.
Gothenburg-Frederikshavn
service.

2 Stena Danica *in the Kattegat.*
(Arnold Kludas.)
3 *The* Stena Jutlandica *on a
shakedown cruise.* (Achim Borchert.)

1 Umsini *was the last in a series of
four passenger ships for Indonesia.*
(Steffen Weirauch.)

1

2

3

Motorship *Stena Scandinavica*
Stena Line A/B, Gothenburg
PoR: ?

Builders: Stocznia im Komuny
Paryskiej, Gdynia
Yard no: 49401
23,000 GRT; 4,500 DWT; 173.0 ×
29.0 m / 566 × 95.1 ft; Four 16-
cyl geared diesels, ZUT Zgoda-
Sulzer; Twin screw; 30,000 kW
(40,000 BHP); 22 kn.

1981 Aug 22: Launched.
Because of political and economic
crisis in Poland, completion and
target delivery date of early 1983
not possible to achieve.
1983 Jun: Stena Line took over
incomplete vessel, to ensure
resumption of building hitherto
delayed as a result of sub-
contractors' reservations regarding
payment.
1985 Stena Line invited European
yards to tender for completion of
Stena Scandinavica and three
sister ships also ordered in Poland.
July 22: Supervision of work taken
over by consulting team of
Swedish engineers. Planned
delivery date: October 1 1986.

Motorship *Stena Germanica*
Stena Line A/B, Gothenburg
PoR: ?

Builders: Stocznia Gdanska,
Gdansk
Yard no: 49402

1983 Apr 16: Launched.
Details as for career to date of
Stena Scandinavica.
Planned delivery date: April 1987

Motorship *Stena—*
Stena Line A/B, Gothenburg

Builders: Stocznia im Komuny
Paryskiej, Gydnia
Yard no: 49403

1985 Procedure as for *Stena
Scandinavica*.

Motorship Stena—
Stena Line A/B, Gothenburg

Builders: Stocznia Gdanska,
Gdansk
Yard no: 49404

1985 Procedure as for *Stena
Scandinavica*.

Turbine steamer *Fairsky*
Sitmar Cruises Inc, Monrovia
PoR: Monrovia

Builders: Constructions Navales &
Industrielles de la Méditerranée,
La Seyne
Yard no: 1436
22,120 GRT; 7,673 DWT; 240.4 ×
27.8 m / 789 × 91.2 ft; Two sets
geared turbines, General Electric
Co; Twin screw; 21,700 kW
(29,500 SHP); 22 kn; Passengers:
1,600; Crew: 563.

1982 Nov 6: Launched for Sitmar
Cruises Inc, Monrovia.
1984 Apr: Delivered.
May 2: Arrived at Los Angeles.
May 5: Naming ceremony.
Cruising on United States market.

1 *The 23,000 GRT* Stena Scandinavica *at her Gdynia fitting-out berth.* (Z. Kosycarz.)

1

2

2 *Launch of the* Stena Germanica. (Janusz Uklejewski.)

3

3 *The* Fairsky *glides down the ways at La Seyne.* (CNIM.)

Motorship *Ankara*
Turkiye Denizcilik Isletmeleri
Istanbul Acentesi, Istanbul
PoR: Istanbul

Builders: Stocznia Szczecinska
im A. Warskiego, Szczecin
Yard no: B490/03
10,552 GRT; 1,750 DWT; 127.4 ×
19.4 m / 417 × 63.6 ft; Four 6-cyl
geared diesels, Zgoda-Sulzer;
Twin screw; 12,360 kW (16,800
BHP); 20.2 kn; Passengers: 460,
plus 523 unberthed; Private cars:
214.

1982 Launched as *Mazowia* for
Polish ownership.
While under construction
transferred to Turkey, payment to
be set against Polish national debt.
1983 Jun: Completed.
Jul 1: Maiden voyage Istanbul-
Izmir service.

Motorship *Samsun*
DB Deniz Nakliyati TAS Genel
Mudurlugu, Turkish Cargo Lines,
Istanbul
PoR: Istanbul

Builders: Stocznia Szczecinska im
A. Warskiego, Szczecin
Yard no: B490/04
10,583 GRT; 1,788 DWT; 127.5 ×
19.4 m / 418 × 63.6 ft; Four 6-cyl
geared diesels, Zgoda-Sulzer;
Twin screw; 12,360 kW (16,800
BHP); 19.5 kn; Passengers: 598,
plus 112 unberthed.

1984 Aug 31: Launched.
1985 Jun: Delivered.
Istanbul-Izmir service.

Motorship *New Yamato*
Hankyu Ferry KK, Shimonoseki
PoR: Shimonoseki

Builders: Kanda Zosensho KK,
Kawajiri
Yard no: 277
11,919 GRT; 4,999 DWT; 173.0 ×
26.8 m / 568 × 87.9 ft; Two 12-
cyl geared diesels,
Maschinenfabirk Augsburg-
Nürnberg-Mitsubishi; Twin screw;
17,650 kW (24,000 BHP); 21 kn,
24.25 on trials; Passengers: 711;
Private cars: 133; Commercial
vehicles: 136.

1983 Oct: Maiden voyage
Kokura-Izumioso.

Motorship *New Miyako*
Hankyu Ferry KK, Shimonoseki
PoR: Shimonoseki

Builders: Kanda Zosensho KK,
Kawajiri
Yard no: 278
11,914 GRT; 5,022 DWT; 173.0 ×
26.8 m / 568 × 87.9 ft; Two 12-
cyl geared diesels,
Maschinenfabrik Augsburg-
Nürnberg-Mitsubishi; Twin screw;
17,650 kW (24,000 BHP); 21 kn;
Passengers: 436, plus 375
unberthed; Private cars: 133;
Commercial vehicles: 136.

1983 Oct 26: Launched.
1984 Delivered. Kokura-Izumioso
service.

1 Samsun *and her sister* Ankara *are
employed along the Turkish coast.*
(Selim San, Weirauch collection.)
2 *The new sisters on the Kokura-
Izumiosu run are the* New Miyako
(illustrated) and the New Yamato.
(Yoshido Ikeda.)

Motorship *Holiday*
Carnival Cruise Lines Inc
(Sunbury Assets Inc), Miami/Fl
PoR: Panama

Builders: Aalborg Vaerft A/S,
Aalborg
Yard no: 246
46,052 GRT; 7,186 DWT; 221.6 ×
28.0 m / 727 × 91.9 ft; Two 7-cyl
diesels, Sulzer Bros; Twin screw;
22,360 kW (20,400 BHP); 21.75
kn; Passengers: 1,800; Crew: 600.

1983 Dec 10: Launched.
1985 Jan: First trials.
Jun 3: Delivered.
Cruising in Caribbean.

Motorship *Champs Elysées*
Soc Nationale des Chemins de Fer
Français (SNCF), Paris
PoR: Dunkirk

Builders: Chantiers Dubigeon SA,
Nantes
Yard no: 167
15,093 GRT; 2,430 DWT; 130.0 ×
22.5 m / 426 × 73.8 ft; Two 16-cyl
geared diesels, Pielstick-Alsthom-
Atlantique; Twin screw; 12,700
kW (17,265 BHP); 18.5 kn;
Passengers: 4, plus 1,800
unberthed; Crew: 84; Private cars:
330, *or* Commercial vehicles: 84.

1983 Dec 21: Launched.
1984 Oct 2: Delivered.
Ferry service, Calais-Dover.

Motorship *Royal Princess*
P&O Steam Navigation Co,
London
PoR: London

Builders: O/Y Wärtsilä A/B,
Helsinki
Yard no: 464
44,348 GRT; 4,661 DWT; 230.6 ×
32.2 m / 757 × 105.6 ft; Four 6-
cyl geared diesels, Pielstick-O/Y
Wärtsilä; Twin screw; 23,200,
29,160 kW max (31,550 BHP); 22
kn; Passengers: 1,260; Crew: 518.

1984 Feb 17: Floated out of
building dock.
Oct 30: Delivered.
Nov 15: Naming ceremony at
Southampton.
Nov 19: Maiden voyage,
positioning, Southampton-Miami,
then cruising on US market.

Motorship *Ferry Lilac*
Shin Nipponkai Ferry KK, Osaka
PoR: Otaru

Builders: Ishikawajima Harima
Heavy Industries, Aioi
Yard no: 2904
18,268 GRT; 8,285 DWT; 192.9 ×
29.4 m / 633 × 96.5 ft; Two 8-cyl
geared diesels, Pielstick-
Ishikawajima; Twin screw; 17,500
kW (23,760 BHP); 21.75 kW
(23,760 BHP); 21.75 kn, 24.87 kn
on trials; Passengers: 544; Crew:
54; Private cars: 136; Commercial
vehicles: 152.

1984 Mar 27: Launched.
Jul 10: Delivered. Then Maizuru-
Otaru service.

Motorship *Mariella*
SF Line A/B (Viking Line),
Mariehamn
PoR: Mariehamn

Builders: O/Y Wärtsilä A/B, Åbo
Yard no: 1286
37,799 GRT; 2,500 DWT; 177.0 ×
28.4 m / 581 × 93.2 ft; Four 12-
cyl geared diesels, Pielstick-
O/Y Wärtsilä; Twin screw; 23,000
kW (31,280 BHP); 22 kn;
Passengers: 2,372, plus 128
unberthed; Crew: 180; Private
cars: 580.

1984 Sep 28: Launched.
1985 May 17: Delivered.
May 18: Maiden voyage Helsinki-
Stockholm.

Motorship *Olympia*
Rederi A/B Slite (Viking Line),
Slite

Builders: O/Y Wärtsilä A/B, Åbo
Sister ship to *Mariella,* for above
owners as partners with SF Line
A/B in Viking Line.
For delivery May 1986.

1 *A model of the Aalborg-built liner*
Holiday *for Carnival Cruise Lines.*
2 *The new flagship of P&O, the* Royal
Princess. *(Wärtsilä.)*
3 *The biggest ferries in the world:*
Mariella *and her sister* Olympia. *(K.
Brzoza.)*

1

2

3

Motorship *Svea*
Siljia Line (O/Y Svea Line
[Finland] A/B), Stockholm
PoR: Stockholm

Builders: O/Y Wärtsilä A/B,
Helsinki
Yard no: 470
33,830 GRT; 3,019 DWT; 168.0 ×
27.6 m / 551 × 90.6 ft; Four
12-cyl geared diesels, Pielstick-
O/Y Wärtsilä; Twin screw; 21,600
kW (30,000 BHP); 22 kn;
Passengers: 1,625, plus 375
unberthed; Crew. 180; Private
cars: 350.

1984 Sept 28: Floated out of
building dock.
1985 May 7: Delivered. Then
Stockholm-Åbo service.

Motorship *Wellamo*
Silja Line (Finska Angfartygs A/B
[EFFOA]), Helsinki

Builders: O/Y Wärtsilä A/B,
Helsinki
Yard no: 471

Sister ship to *Svea,* for above

1 *Artist's impression of the* Caribou,
*new flagship of CN Marine, being
built at K Lauzon.*
2 Svea *and her sister* Wellamo *are the
biggest ships in the Silja fleet.*
(K. Brzoza.)

owners as partners with Johnson
Line in Silja Line.
For delivery late 1985.

Motorship *Caribou*
CN Marine Inc, Halifax/NS

Builders: Davie Shipbuilding Ltd,
Lauzon, PQ
Yard no: 705
13,500 GRT; 179.0 × 25.0 m /587
× 82.0 ft; Four 8-cyl geared
diesels, MaK Maschinenbau; Twin
screw; 20,600 kW (28,000 BHP);
22 kn; Passengers: 196, plus 1,150
unberthed; Private cars: 350.

1984 Oct 25: Launched.
For delivery September 1985.
Nova Scotia-Newfoundland
service.

Motorship *Homeric*
Home Lines Inc (Soc de Gestion
Evge SA, Piraeus)

Builders: Jos. L. Meyer GmbH &
Co, Papenburg
Yard no: 610
42,092 GRT; 5,100 DWT; 204.0 ×
29.0 m / 669 × 95.1 ft; Two
10-cyl diesels; Twin screw; 23,600
kW; 22.5 kn; Passengers: 1,260.

1985 Sep 28: Launched.
Dec 26-30: First trials.
1986 May 6: Delivered. Naming
ceremony at New York.
Cruising, New York-Bermuda
service.

Motorship *Free Enterprise VI*
Townsend Car Ferries Ltd,
Tonbridge
PoR: Dover

Builders: IHC 'Gusto' NV,
Schiedam
Yard no: 881
12,503 GRT; 2,100 DWT; 139.4 ×
22.0 m / 457 × 72.2 ft; Three
12-cyl diesels, Stork-Werkspoor;
Triple screw; 9,270 kW (12,600
BHP); 19 kn; Passengers: 68, plus
1,132 unberthed; Crew: 85;
Private cars: 370; Commercial
vehicles: 60.

1972 Jan 29: Launched.
Jun: Delivered. 4,981 GRT.
Length: 117.5 m (385 ft); breadth:
19.1 m (62.7 ft). 22 kn. Private
cars: 250. Commercial vehicles:
25.
Dover-Zeebrugge service.
1985 Jun: Arrived at
Bremerhaven, Schichau-
Unterweser Werft, where
lengthened and heightened by an
additional deck.
Oct 22: Delivered following
reconstruction. 12,503 GRT.

3 *The* Homeric *after being launched
on September 28 1985.* (Steffen
Weirauch.)
4 Free Enterprise VI *in her new look.*
(Peter Voss.)

1

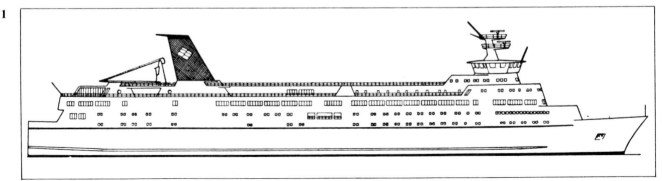

2

3

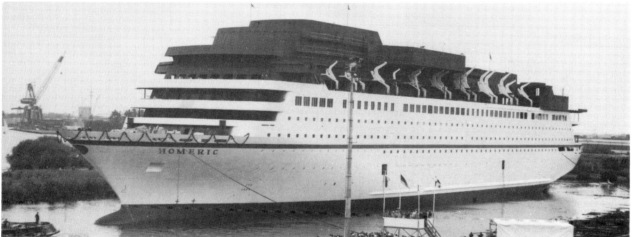

4

Motorship *Birka Princess*
Birka Line A/B, Mariehamn

Builders: Valmet O/Y Helsingen
Telakka (Helsinki Shipyard),
Helsinki
Yard no: 321
21,000 GRT; 143.0 × 24.7 m /469
× 81.0 ft; Four 12-cyl geared
diesels, Pielstick-O/Y Wärtsilä;
Twin screw; 15,500 kW (21,100
BHP); 20 kn; Passengers: 1,500.

1985 Oct 29: Launched.
1986 Delivered.
Stockholm-Mariehamn service and
cruising.

Motorship *Koningin Beatrix*
Stoomvaart Maats Zeeland
(Koninklijke Nederlandsche
Postvaart NV), Hook of Holland

Builders: Van der Giessen-
de Noord BV, Krimpen
Yard no: 935
30,000 GRT; 161.0 × 27.6 m /528
× 90.6 ft; Four 8-cyl diesels,
Maschinenfabrik Augsburg-
Nürnberg; Twin screw; 19,360
kW; 21 kn.

1985 Nov 9: Launched.
1986 Delivered.
Hook of Holland-Harwich
service.

Motorship *Peter Pan*
Travemünde-Trelleborg Linie (TT-
Linie) GmbH & Co, Hamburg

Builders: Seebeckwerft AG,
Bremerhaven
Yard no: 1058
30,000 GRT; 161.0 × 28.0 m /528
× 91.9 ft; Four 8-cyl diesels, MaK
Maschinenbau; Twin screw;
19,600 kW (26,640 BHP); 21 kn;
Passengers: 1,322, plus 378
unberthed; Private cars: 550.

1985 Nov 30: Launched.
1986 May 30: Delivered, then
Travemünde-Trelleborg service.

Motorship *Nils Holgersson*
A/B Swedcarrier (Scandinavian
Ferry Lines A/B, Helsingborg)

Builders: Seebeckwerft AG,
Bremerhaven
Yard no: 1059

Sister ship to *Peter Pan*.
For delivery March 1987.

Motorship *Peder Paars*
Government of the Kingdom of
Denmark (Danske Statsbaner),
Copenhagen
PoR: Aarhus

Builders: A/S Nakskov
Skibsvaerft, Nakskov
Yard no: 233
11,602 GRT; Two 8-cyl diesels,
Maschinenfabrik Augsburg-
Nürnberg-Burmeister & Wain;
Twin screw; 12,480 kW (16,960
BHP); 17 kn; Passengers: 2,000;
Private cars: 331.

1985 Launched.
Nov 19: Delivered. Then Aarhus-
Kalundborg service.

Motorship *Nils Klim*
Government of the Kingdom of
Denmark (Danske Statsbaner),
Copenhagen

Builders: A/S Nakskov
Skibsvaerft, Nakskov
Yard no: 234

1985 May 29: Launched.

Sister ship to *Peder Paars*.
For delivery June 1986.

1

1 Peter Pan *at the fitting out berth in
February 1986.* (Peter Voss.)

2 Celebration *and* Jubilee *are to be the
names of the two ships being built by
Kockums M/V A/B for Carnival
Cruise Lines Inc.*

New construction

A ferry for the Government of the Kingdom of Sweden, Statens Jarnvager Farjedriften, Malmö. Builders: Moss-Rosenberg Verft A/S, Moss. Yard no: 204. 178.0 × 23.0 m / 583 × 75.5 ft. For delivery June 1986.

A ferry for the Government of the Fedcral Republic of Germany (Deutsche Bundesbahn, Bundesbahndirektion, Hamburg). Builders: Howaldtswerke-Deutsche Werft AG, Kiel. Yard no: 211. 13,700 GRT. 164.6 × 17.4 m / 540 × 57.1 ft. 19,000 kW. 18.6 kn. 'D-Zug' waggons: 14. Private cars: 156. For delivery July 1986.

A ferry for Oshima Unyu KK, Naze. Builders: Usuki Tekkosho, Usuki. Yard no: 1328. 16,800 GRT. 19 kn. For delivery August 1986.

Two cruise-ships for Carnival Cruise Lines Inc, Miami / Fl. Builders: Kockums A/B, Malmö. Yard nos: 596 and 597. 45,000 GRT. 224.8 × 28.0 m / 738 × 91.9 ft. 21 kn. For delivery 1986 and 1987. Proposed names: *Celebration* and *Jubilee*. To be similar to same owners' *Holiday*.

A cruise-ship for South African Marine Corp Ltd, Cape Town. Builders: Howaldtswerke-Deutsche Werft AG, Kiel. Yard no: 218. 21,000 GRT. 176.2 × 22.7 m / 578 × 74.5 ft. Named *Astor* in ceremony on Jun 24. For delivery January 1987.

A ferry for Anders Jahre, Sandefjord. Builders: O/Y Wärtsilä A/B, Åbo. Yard no: 1292. 27,000 GRT. 164.5 × 28.4 m / 540 × 93.2 ft. For delivery March 1987. Passengers: 1,500. Private cars: 283. Commercial vehicles: 73.

A ferry for Hollandsche Vrachtvaart Maats BV (North Sea Ferries), Rotterdam. Builders: Nippon Kokan KK, Tsurumi. Yard no: T 1033. 31,000 GRT. 179.0 × 25.4 m / 587 × 83.3 ft. 18 kn. Rotterdam-Hull service. Launched as *Norsun*, Sep 1986. For delivery April 1987.

A ferry for North Sea Ferries Ltd, Hull. Builders: Govan Shipbuilders Ltd, Glasgow. Yard no: 265. 31,000 GRT. 179.0 × 25.3 m / 587 × 83.0 ft. 18 kn. Hull-Rotterdam service. Launched as *Norsea*, Sep 9 1986. For delivery 1987.

A ferry for Soc Nationale des Chemins de Fer Français, Paris. Builders: Chantiers de France-Dunkerque, Dunkirk. For delivery June 1987.

Two ferries for European Ferries group. Builders: Schichau-Unterweser Werft, Bremerhaven. Yard nos: 2293 and 2294. 20,000 GRT. 22 kn. Names: *Pride of Calais* and *Pride of Dover*. For delivery March and August 1987.

A cruise-ship for Royal Caribbean Cruise Line A/S, Oslo. Builders: Alsthom-Atlantique, St Nazaire. Yard no: A 29. 70,000 GRT. 266.5 × 32.2 m / 874 × 105. 6 ft. For delivery December 1987. *Sovereign of the Seas*.

Two cruise-ships for Contessa Cruise Line Inc, Houston/Tex. Builders: Marine Power & Equipment Co Inc, Seattle/Wash. 18,000 GRT. 165.0 × 24.4 m / 541 × 80.0 ft. Passengers: 800. Crew: 300. For delivery 1987.

Two cruise-ships for Royal Cruise Line Ltd, Piraeus. Builders: Jos. L. Meyer GmbH & Co, Papenburg. Yard nos: 616 and 617. 40,000 GRT. 187.0 × 28.2 m / 614 × 92.5 ft. 22 kn. For delivery June and December 1988. Proposed names: *Crown Odyssey* and *Golden Odyssee*.

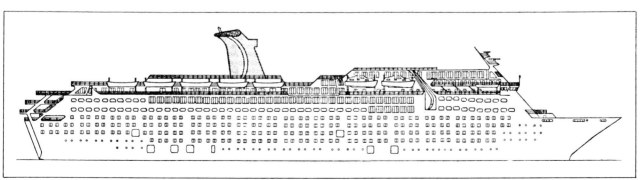

Appendix 1: Former great passenger ships

This appendix updates the careers of those ships featured in volumes 1 to 5 of *Great Passenger Ships of the World* still in existence but which in 1985 either no longer carried passengers or had been remeasured at less than 10,000 GRT. All changes since 1976 are noted. The figures following each ship name are the volume and page number wherein the earlier career of the ship in question can be found (eg, 5/124 indicates volume 5, page 124). For ease of reference ships are listed by their original names, in alphabetical order.

Admiral C.F. Hughes 4/128
Currently laid up as *General Edwin D. Patrick.*

Admiral E.W. Eberle 4/126
Currently laid up as *General Simon B. Buckner.*

Admiral H.T. Mayo 4/128
Currently laid up as *General Nelson M. Walker.*

Admiral Hugh Rodman 4/130
Currently laid up as *General Maurice Rose.*

Admiral R.E. Coontz 4/126
Currently laid up as *General Alexander M. Patch.*

Admiral W.L. Capps 4/124
Currently laid up as *General Hugh J. Gaffey.*

Admiral W.S. Benson 4/124
Currently laid up as *General Daniel I. Sultan.*

Admiral W.S. Sims 4/130
Currently laid up as *General William O. Darby.*

Amelia de Mello 5/162
1979 To Cia de Vapores Realma SA, Panama, as *Dolphin IV.* 8,854 GRT; 4,036 DWT.

America 4/84
1977 Nov 18: Final departure from Southampton.
1978 Sold to America Cruise Lines, Panama, whose name then changed to Ventura Cruise Lines.

May 19: Arrived at New York. Renamed *America.*
Jun 30: First cruise following refit, to Martha's Vineyard Island, Mass.
Jul 20: Organisational breakdown forced Venture Cruise Lines to abandon operations.
Aug: Ship returned to Chandris. Okeanis SA, Panama. Renamed *Italis.*
1979 After general refit which included removal of fore funnel, *Italis* cruised in Mediterranean from middle of year.
Sep 12: Laid up at Pireaus.
1980 May: Sold to Intercommerce Corp SA, subsidiary of Cia Noga d'Importation & d'Exportation, Panama, backed by Swiss interests. Renamed *Noga,* equipped as hotel.
1984 Renamed *Alferdoss.* Registered under ownership of Silvermoon Ferries Ltd.

1 *Renamed* Noga *and laid up, the former* America. *(Weirauch collection.)*

1

Anna Nery 5/135
1978 Sold to Kavounides Hellenic Cruises. Renamed *Danaos*. Laid up at Piraeus. To Kavolines Corp SA, Piraeus, as *Constellation*. Remained laid up.
1981 Nov: To Kaohsiung for refitting by China Shipbuilding Co.
1982 May 12: Refit completed. Jun: Cruising in Mediterranean.
1984 7,952 GRT.
1985 Kavounides Shipping Co SA Ltd, Piraeus.
Oct: Laid up at Piraeus.

Augustus 5/8
1976 Sold to Great Shipping & Investment Ltd and registered at Port Victoria, Seychelles. Renamed *Great Sea*. To Hong Kong for refit.
1977 Jul: To Keelung for further refitting. Transferred to Great Sea Shipping Co, Panama.
Oct 17: Arrived at Hong Kong and laid up there.
1978 Jul 3: One voyage to

Kaohsiung and Keelung.
Aug 21: Again laid up at Hong Kong.
1980 Sold to Ocean King Navigation Co, Manila. Renamed *Ocean King*.
1982 Jan 14: Laid up at Manila.
1983 Renamed *Philippines*. Accommodation ship at Manila.
1985 Renamed *President*.

Aurelia 5/74
(Ex *Huascaran*, 6,951 GRT)
1977 Registered in Panama as *Romanza*. 7,538 GRT.
1979 To Armadora Romanza SA, Panama.

Aureol 5/28
1979 Feb: Arrived at Piraeus as *Marianna VI*.
1980 Feb 24: Arrived at Rabegh. Hotel ship. John S. Latsis, Athens.

Boheme 5/172
1970 10,328 GRT following reconstruction by Blohm + Voss AG, Hamburg. Passengers: 504.
1981 Sold to Sally Shipping

GmbH, Bad Schwartau.
Mar: Sally Shipping subsidiary, Hanseatic Caribbean Shipping Co Inc, Panama.
1984 7,056 GRT.

Brazil Maru 5/88
Currently museum and restaurant ship at Toba, Ise Bay.

Charlesville 4/182
1977 Sep: Stationed on River Warnow at Rostock-Schmarl as *Georg Büchner*. Shore-based training centre.

Danae 5/204
(Ex cargo liner *Port Melbourne*)
1979 Chartered for five years to Costa Armatori SpA (Linea 'C'), Genoa, as *Danae*.
1985 Sold to Costa Armatori SpA (Linea 'C'), Genoa. Registered under ownership of Independent Continental Lines Ltd, Panama. Cruising in American waters. 9,603 GRT.

1 *The* Danae *arriving at Bremerhaven.* (Peter Voss.)

2

Daphne 5/204
(Ex cargo liner *Port Sydney*)
1979 Chartered for three years to
Costa Armatori SpA (Linea 'C'),
Genoa, as *Daphne*. Later extended
to five years.
1983 11,683 GRT.
1985 Sold to Costa Armatori SpA
(Linea 'C'), Genoa. Registered
under ownership of Independent
Continental Lines Ltd, Panama.
Cruising in American waters.
9,436 GRT.

Empress of Australia 5/151
1973 8,196 GRT.
1985 Sold to Phineas Navigation
Ltd, Limassol. Renamed *Empress*.

Frederick Funston 4/93
Currently laid up.

Freeport I 5/167
1976 Nov: 9,908 GRT.
1981 Mar: To Panamanian flag as
Caribe Bremen. To DFDS
Seaways (Bahamas) Ltd, Nassau.
Renamed *Scandinavian Sun*.
Nov: Refitted by Howaldtswerke-
Deutsche Werft AG, Hamburg,
for one-day cruises.
1982 Jan: Miami-Freeport service.
1984 Aug 20: Fire on board while
at Miami. Three dead.

General A.E. Anderson 4/114
1958 Dec 11: Removed from US
Navy List. Currently laid up.
Believed sold to Taiwan breakers.

General A.W. Brewster 4/110
Currently in service as
Philadelphia.

General C.H. Muir 4/108
Currently in service as *San Juan*.

General D.E. Aultman 4/110
In service as *Portland*.
1986 Oct: Reported sold, possibly
for breaking up.

General Harry Taylor 4/98
Currently in service as *General
Hoyt S. Vandenberg*.

General H.B. Freeman 4/108
In service as *Newark*.
1986 Oct: Reported sold, possibly
for breaking up.

General J.C. Breckinridge 4/122
Currently laid up.

General J.H. McRae 4/102
1982 *Amco Voyager*. Merchant
Terminal Corp, New York.
1985 Apr 19: Laid up at New
York.

General John Pope 4/114
1969 Laid up in Suisun Bay by US
Maritime Administration.

Général Mangin 5/70
1977 To Bangladesh Shipping
Corp, Chittagong. Renamed
Hizbul Bahr. 11,684 GRT.
Chittagong-Dubai service.
1980 Dec 11: Final arrival at
Chittagong from Dubai.
1981 To Bangladesh Navy as
Shaheed Salahuddin.

General M.B. Stewart 4/106
Drilling vessel. *Mission Viking*.
1976 To Mission Drilling &
Exploration Corp, later Mission
Viking Inc, New Orleans.
1981 Manufacturers' Hanover
Leasing Corp, Panama.

General M.L. Hersey 4/100
Currently in service as *St Louis*.

General R.E. Callan 4/102
Currently in service as *General
H.H. Arnold*.

General W.A. Mann 4/116
Currently laid up.

General W.G. Haan 4/112
1982 *Amco Trader*. Merchant

Terminal Corp, New York.
1985 Apr 19: Laid up at New
York.

General W.H. Gordon 4/118
Currently laid up.

General William Mitchell 4/116
Currently laid up.

General William Weigel 4/122
Currently laid up.

Hikawa Maru 3/132
Currently at Yokohama.

Infante Dom Henrique 5/130
1977 Nov 25: Sold to Cabinete da
Area de Sines.
Moored behind protective
embankment as accommodation
ship at Sines.

James O'Hara 4/93
Currently laid up.

Jean Laborde 5/56
Planned conversion to car ferry,
1973/74 (to have included
renaming as *Brindisi Express*), did
not take place.
1974 *Eastern Princess*.
Efthymiadis subsidiary Helite
Hellenic Italian Lines SA,
Panama.
Sep: Piraeus-Far East, then
Singapore-Australia service.
1976 *Oceanos*. Pontos Naviera
SA, Panama. 7,554 GRT.
Mediterranean cruising.
1981 To Hellenic Co for Sea &
Waterways SA, Piraeus
(Epirotiki).

Marine Adder 4/140
1985 Apr 28: Laid up at
Jacksonville as *Transcolorado*.

Marine Cardinal 4/132
(See also Appendix 2)
1970 As *Baltimore*, after section

1 *The floating restaurant* Hikawa
Maru *at Yokohama.* (Weirauch
collection.)

2 *The* Oceanos, *ex* Jean Laborde, *was
another passenger vessel to have her
tonnage reduced. In 1976 it fell by 25
per cent.* (Peter Voss.)

joined to newly-constructed forward section to form container ship *San Pedro*. Currently in service.

Marine Falcon 4/134
1977 *Borinquen*. Puerto Rico Maritime Shipping Authority, San Juan, PR.

Marine Flasher 4/134
Currently in service as *Long Beach*.

Marine Jumper 4/134
Currently in service as *Panama*.

Marine Lynx 4/138
1985 Aug 23: Laid up at San Francisco as *Transcolumbia*.

Marine Serpent 4/136
Currently in service as *Galveston*.

Marine Shark 4/132
1984 Feb: Laid up at New York as *Charleston*.

1986 Oct: Sold to United States breakers.

Marine Tiger 4/132
Currently in service as *Oakland*.

Michelangelo 5/142
Currently Iranian Navy accommodation ship.

Monte Granada 5/190
1977 Sold to Libyan Ministry of Transport (General National Maritime Transport Co, Tripoli). Renamed *Garnata*. 6,626 GRT.

Monte Toledo 5/190
1977 Sold to Libyan Ministry of Transport (General National Maritime Transport Co, Tripoli). Renamed *Toletela*. 6,634 GRT.

Ohrmazd 5/158
1971 Not used as passenger vessel since Indo-Pakistani war.

President Hayes 4/226
Currently in service as *State of Main*.

President Jackson 4/226
Currently in service as *Empire State V*.

Pretoria 4/22
1979 To Indonesian Navy. Renamed *Tanjung Pandan*. Accommodation ship at Tanjung Priok.

Principe Perfeito 5/130
1980 Sold to Fair Line Shipping Corp, Panama. Renamed *Fairsky*. Jan 20: Laid up at Itea, Greece.
1981 Renamed *Vera*.
1982 Sold to Sapho Shipping & Trading Corp, Panama. Renamed *Marianna IX*.
Jun 30: Arrived at Jeddah.
Dec: Arrived at Rabegh, Saudi Arabia, for use as accommodation ship.

1

Queen Mary 3/216
Currently at Long Beach.

Raffaello 5/142
Currently Iranian Navy
accommodation ship.
1982 Nov 20-21: According to
press reports heavily damaged and
set on fire in neighbourhood of
Bushire by Iraqi air attack.

Renaissance 5/140
1977 To Epirotiki Lines SA,
Piraeus, as *Homeric Renaissance*.

1978 To Hellenic Co Overseas
Cruises SA (Epirotiki), Piraeus.
Renamed *World Renaissance*.
1979 8,665 GRT.
1983 Aug: Chartered by St Helena
Shipping Co for operation by
Curnow Shipping Ltd,
Porthleven, Cornwall. Plymouth-
Tenerife-St Helena-Cape Town
service. Also cruising in South
African waters.
1985 Returned to Mediterranean
cruising.

Rosa da Fonseca 5/135
1977 Sold to Mitsui OSK Lines
Ltd, Tokyo. Renamed *Nippon
Maru*. 9,745 GRT.

1 *The* State of Maine, *ex* President
Hayes. (Steven Lang.)
2 *For the time being a memorial to a
past era: the* Queen Mary *at Long
Beach*. (Martin Lochte-Holtgreven.)
3 *As the* Nippon Maru *the* Rosa de
Fonseca *falls just below the tonnage
threshold*. (Weirauch collection.)

2

3

Ryndam 5/36
1981 To Hellenic Co for Mediterranean Cruises SA (Epirotiki), Piraeus. Renamed *Atlas*. 9,114 GRT.

San Lorenzo 5/40
Currently does not carry passengers.

Santa Mercedes 5/138
Following amalgamation of Grace Line Inc and Prudential Line Inc to form Prudential-Grace Lines Inc, service from Vancouver, BC, through Panama Canal encircling South America and returning to Vancouver having called at 20 intermediate ports.
1982 Sold to Delta Steamship Lines Inc, New Orleans.
1984 Sold to US Maritime Commission for use as training ship for Massachusetts Maritime Academy. Renamed *Patriot State*. Jun 14: Arrived at San Francisco for fitting out.

Santa Paula 5/112
1978 Sep 24: To Kuwait following further conversion at Rijeka.
Oct 17: Raising of bed of harbour at ship's berth commenced. Hull to remain permanently grounded.
1980 Feb 1: Opened as *Kuwait Mariott Hotel*.

Savannah 5/126
1981 Opened as museum-ship at Patriot Point, Charleston, SC.

Stockholm 4/158
1974 As *Völkerfreundschaft,* owners styled VEB Deutfracht/Seereederei. 11,970 GRT.
1985 Apr: Decommissioned at Rostock.
Jul: Reported sold on undisclosed terms.
Dec 11: Arrived at Southampton.
1986 Dec 18: Left Southampton for Norway as *Fridtjof Nansen*.

Victoria 5/18
1974 Passengers: 430 in one class.
1977 Jan 14: Laid up.
1978 Purchased by American 'Youth with a Mission' organisation for use as floating church. Registered at Limassol, Cyprus, under ownership of YWAM Shipping Co. Renamed *Anastasis*.
1979 Jul 5: Laid up at Piraeus.
1982 To Maritime Mercy Ministries Ltd, Malta.

Windsor Castle 5/114
1977 To Margarita Shipping & Trading Corp, Panama (John S. Latsis), as *Margarita L*.
Oct 9: Arrived at Piraeus for work to commence on conversion to floating luxury hotel at Jeddah.
1979 Jan 11: Permanently moored at Jeddah.
1984 Registered under ownership of Santa Marianna Shipping & Trading Corp SA, Panama.

1

1 *The 9,114 GRT* Atlas, *ex* Ryndam. (Ralf Witthohn.)

2 *The* Anastasis, *ex* Victoria. (Weirauch collection.)

3 *The* Margarita L *immediately after renaming, but still flying the Union-Castle flag of her* Windsor Castle *days.* (Weirauch collection.)

Appendix 2: Passenger ships withdrawn between 1976 and 1986

This appendix completes the biographies of those ships featured in volumes 1 to 5 of *Great Passenger Ships of the World* which have since ceased to exist. All changes in respect of each ship are given up to the date of sale to breakers or loss through accident. The figures following each ship name are the volume and page numbers wherein the earlier career of the ship in question can be found. For ease of reference ships are listed by their original name in alphabetical order.

Africa 5/16
1980 Mar 25: Left Trieste for breakers at Kaohsiung as *Protea*.
May 17: Breaking up commenced by Nan Yet Steel Enterprises.

Albert Ballin 2/216
1980 Renamed *Soyuz*.
1981 Reported broken up.

Alberto Dodero 5/32
1980 Sold to Ahmed Awad Etaiwi, Jeddah. Renamed *Etaiwi 1*.
1983 Etaiwi Shipping Co, Jeddah.
1985 Aug 28: To breakers at Kaohsiung, Taiwan.

Alfonso XIII 2/152
1978 Broken up in Spain as *Galicia*.

Amazon 5/122
1977 Owned by Sagitta Ltd, Monrovia, as *Hual Akarita*.
1980 Renamed *Akarita* again, registered under ownership of Ace Autoline Co, Monrovia.
1981 To breakers at Kaohsiung at end of year.

Aragon 5/124
1977 To Ace Navigation Co, Monrovia as *Hual Traveller*.

1980 Renamed *Traveller*.
1981 Oct 29: From New Orleans to Kaohsiung, where broken up by Chien Yu Steel Industrial Co.

Arcadia 5/24
1979 Feb 22: Arrived at Kaohsiung to be broken up.
Feb 28: Breaking up commenced by Lee Chong Steel & Iron Works.

Arlanza 5/124
1977 To Ace Navigation Co, Monrovia as *Hual Trotter*.
1980 Renamed *Trotter*.
1981 To breakers at Kaohsiung at end of year.

Asia 5/18
1977 Completion of rebuilding as livestock transport.
1984 Sold to Norleb Shipping Enterprises Sarl, Beirut. Renamed *Norleb*.
1985 To breakers in Pakistan.
Dec 10: Arrived at Gadoni Beach.

Australia 5/13
1977 Jul 4: As *Donizetti,* breaking up commenced by Cantiere Navale del Golfo, La Spezia.

Bergensfjord 5/102
1977 18,595 GRT.
1978 Jun: Laid up at Singapore.
Nov: To Sunlit Cruises, Limassol, as *Golden Moon*.
Dec 11: Arrived at Perama for refit.
1980 Resold to Greek Aphrodite Maritime Co while refitting. Renamed *Rasa Sayang* again.
Aug 27: Fire which broke out in engine room could not be controlled. Towed out to Kynosoura and there run ashore. Later capsized. Broken up on spot.

Berlin 3/44
1986 Sep 1: As *Admiral Nakhimov* sank in Black Sea following collision with *Pyotr Vasev*. 398 dead.

Biloxi 4/90
1974 Renamed *Bay State,* Massachusetts Maritime Academy.
1979 Transferred to Department of Commerce.
1981 Jul: Reported sold to Tampa Barge Services Inc, but transaction did not proceed.
1982 Jan: Sold by US Maritime Administration to Union Minerals & Alloys Corp, New York, 'for non-transport or scrapping use'. Jan 19: Arrived at Kearny, NJ, to be broken up.

Cabo San Roque 5/92
1977 Jan 24: Badly damaged by fire at Ferrol.
Apr 1: To Growth Maritime Investments Ltd who had ship renamed *Golden Moon* and towed to Piraeus for repair. 14,182 GRT.
1978 Sold to Government of Cuba and registered under ownership of Empress Naviera Mambisa, Havana, as *Africa-Cuba*.
Jul: Laid up at Mariel.
1982 Jul 26: Arrived in tow at Barcelona, where broken up.

Cabo San Vicente 5/92
1984 Feb 16: Laid up at Bombay.
1985 Broken up as *Noor Jehan*.

Campana 3/142
1975 A report that ship left Barcelona for La Spezia on November 29 to be broken up proved incorrect.
1981 Taken out of service following inspection by Italian classification society RINA.

1983 Sep 5: As *Irpinia,* breaking up commenced by Cantiere Navale 'Santa Maria', La Spezia.

Caribia 3/206
1983 Jul: Supplement No 1 to Lloyd's Register 1983/84 notes *Ilyich* as 'no longer seagoing' and therefore to be erased from Register.

Charles Tellier 4/200
1967 To Perusahaan Pelajaran Arafat PT, Jakarta. 12,177 GRT.
1978 Returned to Cia de Navegacion Abeto SA.
Mar 28: Laid up at Jakarta.
1984 Jun 17: Arrived at Chittagong as *Le Havre Abeto,* where broken up by Diamond Steel Products.

Cilicia 4/40
1980 Aug 8: Renamed *Cilicia* again, towed by Dutch tug *Zwarte Zee* to Bilbao where broken up.

City of Port Elizabeth 5/66
1975 *Mediterranean Sun,* Occidental Ultramar SA, Piraeus. Decision whether to rebuild as cruise-ship or car ferry adjourned until 1977. Then laid up.
1980 Registered under ownership of Michael A. Karageorgis.
Mar 12: Left Piraeus for Kaohsiung in tow of Dutch tug *Amsterdam.*
Jun 3: Breaking up commenced by Long Jong Industry Co Ltd.

Claude Bernard 4/198
1979 To Estrella Christal Nav Co, Panama, as *Sunrise IV.*
1980 Jan 3: Laid up at Colombo. Renamed *Pegancia* but never in service under this name.
1981 Apr 28: Left Colombo in tow for Karachi, where broken up.

Clement Ader 5/64
1978 Dec 16: Laid up at Trieste.
1979 Registered under ownership of Sidermar SpA, Trieste.
Aug 22: As *Alessandro Volta,* left Trieste for La Spezia where broken up.

Cordillera 3/208
1979 Feb 10: As *Russ,* breaking up commenced by Han Sung Salvage Co, Inchon.

Cristobal 4/64
1981 Sep: Final voyage.
Nov 10: Sold by Maritime Administration to Consolidated Andy Inc, Brownsville, Tex, for breaking up.

Cristoforo Colombo 5/10
1977 May: Hotel ship at Puerto Ordaz, Venezuela.
1980 Advertised for sale by owners, CVG Siderurgica del Orinoco CA, Ciudad Bolivar.
1981 Mar 12: In tow for Taiwan, broke loose off mouth of Orinoco River but line reconnected.
Jun 30: Arrived at Kaohsiung. Laid up.
1982 May 17: Laid up at Hong Kong.
1983 Jul: Again passenger and cargo vessel. Superluck Enterprises Inc, Panama.
Jul 23: Arrived at Kaohsiung where broken up.

1 *Broken up in 1984,* Le Havre Abeto, *ex* Charles Tellier. (Graf collection.)

1

Cunard Ambassador 5/178
1980 To Lembu Shipping Corp, Panama, as *Procyon*.
1983 *Raslan*. Qatar Transport & Marine Services Co Ltd, Doha.
Jul 3: On voyage Jeddah-Singapore, fire in engine-room control-room.
Jul 17: Laid up at Singapore.
1984 Sep 7: Arrived at Kaohsiung where broken up.

Diemerdyk 4/225
1979 Jun 30: As *Oriental Amiga*, arrived at Kaohsiung where broken up by Chi Young Steel Enterprises.

Dinteldyk 5/106
1976 Transferred to Oriental Central America Lines.
1979 Jan 1: As *Hong Kong Success*, arrived at Kaohsiung where broken up.

Edinburgh Castle 4/184
1976 Jun 4: At Chou's Iron & Steel Co, Kaohsiung, for breaking up.

Edouard Branly 5/62
1977 Transferred to Lloyd Triestino SpA di Navigazione, Trieste.
1978 Oct 23: Laid up at Trieste.
1979 To Italian Lines International SpA.
Feb 24: As *Antonio Pacinotti*, arrived at La Spezia where broken up.

Empress of England 5/96
1975 Jul 17: As *Ocean Monarch*, at Chi Shun Hera Steel Co, Kaohsiung, for breaking up.

Ernie Pyle 4/136
1978 Nov 16: As *Green Lake*, arrived at Kaohsiung where broken up.

Fairsky 5/76
(ex cargo liner *Steel Artisan*)
1977 Jun 26: Run aground off Indonesian coast following collision with sunken wreck.
Dec 18: To Hong Kong where sold to Fuji Marden & Co for breaking up.
1978 Resold to Peninsula Tourist Shipping Corp, Manila, for use as floating hotel.
1979 Nov 3: Caught fire and totally destroyed.

1980 May 24: As *Fair Sky* arrived in tow at Hong Kong where wreck broken up by Fuji Marden & Co.

General A.W. Greeley 4/108
1979 Renamed *Pacific Enterprise*. Austral Glade Owners Ltd, San Francisco.
1982 As *Caribe Enterprise*, Vanessa Trading Co Inc, New York.
1983 May 19: Laid up at New York. To breakers.

General C.C. Ballou 4/112
1981 To Eastern Star Maritime Ltd, Panama. Renamed *Eastern Light*.
Dec 24: Left Kobe for Kaohsiung where broken up.

General C.G. Morton 4/102
1980 Apr 12: As *Green Wave*, breaking up commenced by Sing Cheng Yung Iron & Steel Co, Kaohsiung.

1 *The former* Cunard Ambassador *at Hamburg during her rebuilding as a livestock transport.* (Arnold Kludas.)

General E.T. Collins 4/100
1981 *Eastern Kin,* United Southern Shipping Ltd, Panama.
1982 Jan 9: During voyage New York-Mizushima in bad weather fracture developed in hull. Ship eventually sank 32° 53′N—157° 37′E. Crew rescued.

General G.O. Squier 4/94
1976 To Alpine Steamship Co Inc, New York, as *Penn.*
1978 *Penny.* American Coastal & Foreign Shipping Inc, New York.
1982 Feb 3: Laid up at Tampa.
1983 Nov 30: Grounded in Durban harbour entrance on voyage to Pakistani breakers.
Dec 14: To Mombasa.
1984 Aug: Broken up at Mombasa.

General H.F. Hodges 4/110
1979 Jun 24: As *James,* to Keun Hwa Iron & Steel Works & Enterprises, Kaohsiung, for breaking up.

General H.W. Butner 4/116
1976 Nov 17: Sold to Luris Bros, Brownsville, Tex, for breaking up.

General J.R. Brooke 4/94
1976 To Marlin Steamship Co, Wilmington, Del, renamed *Marlin.* In same year renamed *Mary.*
1979 May 5: Sold for breaking up at Kaohsiung.

General Le Roy Eltinge 4/106
1980 Apr 13: As *Robert Toombs* breaking up commenced by Chien Yu Steel Enterprises, Kaohsiung.

General O.H. Ernst 4/96
1977 Oct 22: Laid up at Cabedello.
1978 Sep 15: As *Orinoco* arrived at Brownsville, Tex, where broken up by Consolidated Andy Inc.

General Omar Bundy 4/104
1976 To Asbury Steamship Co, Wilmington, Del, as *Port.*
1979 Sold to Hawaiian Eugenia Corp, New York. Renamed *Poet.*
1980 Oct 24: Sailed from Philadelphia for Port Said. Did not arrive. Missing since.

General R.L. Howze 4/96
1979 To Austral Glade Owners Ltd, San Francisco, Cal, as *Pacific*

Endeavour.
1981 Broken up in Pakistan.

General R.M. Blatchford 4/106
1979 To US Department of Commerce.
1980 Apr 13: As *Alex Stephens* breaking up commenced by Chien Yu Steel Enterprises, Kaohsiung.

General S.D. Sturgis 4/98
1980 Feb 1: As *Green Port* breaking up commenced by Hua Ling Enterprises, Kaohsiung.

General Stuart Heintzelmann 4/112
1983 Oct 11: Laid up at Hong Kong.
1984 Jul 1: As *Mobile* arrived at Inchon, where broken up by Han Sung Salvage Co.

General W.C. Langfitt 4/104
1978 Nov 5: Laid up at New York.
1983 As *Transindiana* to Brownsville, Tex, where broken up.

2 The *Mobile, ex* General Stuart Heintzelmann, *has since been broken up.* (Hans-Joachim Reinecke.)

2

General W.F. Hase 4/100
1981 *Point Manatee.* Point Vigilance Corp, New York.
1983 Oct: Laid up at Jacksonville, Florida.
1984 Nov: Sold by auction to American buyers. Resold to Hong Kong buyers.
1985 To breakers.

General W.M. Black 4/96
1980 Jan 16: As *Green Forest* breaking up commenced by Sing Cheng Yung Iron & Steel Co, Kaohsiung.

Hamburg 2/222
1976 Out of service.
1977 Broken up as *Yuri Dolgoruki.*

Henri-Poincaré 5/64
1977 Transferred to Lloyd Triestino SpA di Navigazione.
1978 Oct 21: Laid up at Trieste.
1979 Jan 20: As *Galileo Ferraris* towed to La Spezia, where broken up by Cantieri Navali Santa Maria.

Highland Princess 3/114
As *Guanghua,* unofficially reported 1980/81 to have been broken up.

Jadotville 5/104
1975 Nov: As *Chitral* broken up at Kaohsiung by Chou's Iron & Steel Corp.

Kungsholm 5/79
1981 Oct: To Independent Continental Lines Ltd, Panama, subsidiary of Costa Armatori SpA. Renamed *Columbus C.*
Dec 18: First cruise from Buenos Aires, but cruising mainly in European waters.
1984 Jul 29: Struck breakwater and holed while entering Cadiz in bad weather. Sank at berth, resting on bottom. Passengers disembarked.
Sep 14: Declared constructive total loss.
Nov 2: Raised by salvage organisation Smit Tak International, Rotterdam.

1985 Mar: Sold to Spanish breakers.

Laënnec 4/200
1976 To Perusahaan Pelayaran Arafat PT, Jakarta.
Jul 30: As *Belle Abeto,* badly damaged by fire at Sasebo and sank following day.

Laos 5/60
1977 Jun 12: Left Port Kelang in tow for Singapore for breaking up. Resold to breakers at Kaohsiung.
Jul 7: As *Malaysia Raya* breaking up commenced by Kuo Dar Steel & Iron Enterprise.

1 *The final appearance of* Columbus C. (Peter Voss.)
2 *In 1976 the* Belle Abeto, *ex* Laënnec, *was burnt out.* (Bill Miller collection.)

1

Leonardo da Vinci 5/12
1977 Transferred to Italia Crociere Internationali SpA. Cruising.
1978 Sep 23: Laid up at La Spezia.
1980 Jul 3: Caught fire. Towed from harbour. Completely burnt out. Sank in shallow water.
1981 Mar 31: Raised by salvage organisation Smit Tak International, Rotterdam.
1982 May 6: Breaking up commenced by Cantieri Navali Lotti, La Spezia.

Louis Lumière 5/62
1977 Returned to Cia de Navegacion Abeto SA.
Jul 27: Laid up at Jakarta.
1984 Broken up at Chittagong as *Mei Abeto*.

Malolo 3/70
1973 Nov 5: Laid up at Piraeus.
1977 As *Vasilissa Freideriki/ Queen Frederica* breaking up commenced at Elefsis.
1978 Feb 1: Destroyed by fire during course of work.

Marine Cardinal 4/132
(See also Appendix 1)
1970 As *Baltimore,* forward

section joined to after section of tanker *Roanoke* to form container ship *Baltimore*.
1985 Feb: To breakers in Taiwan.

Marine Carp 4/136
1979 Aug 6: As *Green Springs* breaking up commenced by Chin Ho Fa Steel & Iron Co, Kaohsiung.

Marine Perch 4/140
1978 Jun 13: As *Yellowstone* bound from Comean Bay to Tunis, in collision with Algerian motorship *Ibn Batouta* 77 nautical miles southeast of Gibraltar, and sank in position 35°44′N—03° 51′W.

Marine Phoenix 4/138
1979 Sep 16: As *Mohawk* arrived at Kaohsiung where broken up.

Marine Swallow 4/140
1977 To Linnet Shipping Co, Panama. Renamed *Linnet*.
1978 Mar 4: Arrived at Kaohsiung where broken up.

Mikhail Lermontov 5/150
1982 Jan 6: Arrived at Hapag-Lloyd yard, Bremerhaven, for

improvements to or renewal of passenger accommodation. Hull painted white.
May 21: Work completed.
1986 Feb 16: On cruise from Sydney, NSW, struck rocks off South Island, New Zealand, and sank near Port Gore. One crew member missing.

Monte Ulia 5/41
1977 Apr 3: Burnt out at Belfast.
Jun 7: As *Climax Opal* arrived at Santander where broken up by Recuperaçiones Submarines SA.

Monte Urbasa 4/144
(ex cargo liner *Escorial*)
1977 Sold to Specova Naviera SA, Cyprus. Renamed *Esperos I*. Passed on to Sea Manager Navigation Co. In same year resold within Cyprus to Riviera Navigation Co. Renamed *Eurostar*.
1978 Jan: Sold to A.H. Muktar, Beirut, to be broken up.

Nelly 4/223
(ex cargo liner *Mormacmail*)
1977 May 4: As *Seven Seas* from Rotterdam to Belgium, where broken up.

Niassa 5/83
1978 Mar 4: Laid up at Lisbon.
1979 May 13: Arrived at Bilbao in tow. Broken up there.

Ocean Endurance 5/158
1971 Not used as passenger vessel subsequent to India-Pakistan war.
1984 Apr 2: Arrived at Karachi where broken up.

Ocean Monarch 5/26
1971 Laid up at Perama.
1979 To Dolphin (Hellas) Shipping SA, Piraeus. Renamed *Riviera*. Intended for cruising from Venice following refit at Perama. During refit renamed *Reina del Mar*.
1981 May 28: Caught fire shortly before completion of refit. Towed from Perama Harbour and run aground off Salamina.
May 29: Refloated by tug *Titan* and towed half a nautical mile away from the shore. Burnt out and sank there on June 1.

Oceania 5/14
1977 Jun 23: As *Verdi* breaking up commenced by Terestre Marittima, La Spezia.

Oranje 4/60
1976 Sep 18: Laid up at La Spezia.
1977 Chartered to Costa Armatori SpA, Genoa. Renamed *Angelina*. Cruising, Central America.
1979 Mar 30: As *Angelina Lauro*, caught fire at Charlotte Amalie, St Thomas Island, and flooded at berth following day. Total loss.

Panama 4/62
1977 Ownership transferred to Armadora Regina Prima SA, Panama.
1979 Sep 11: Laid up at Piraeus.
1985 10,972 GRT. 6,921 DWT. Dec 4: As *Regina Prima* arrived in tow at Aliaga-Izmir, where broken up.

Pasteur 4/46
1977 Nov 1: Arrived at Jeddah where taken over by Philippine Singapore Ports Corp as accommodation ship for Philippine workers. Renamed *Saudiphil 1*.
1980 To Philsimport International (Hong Kong) Ltd as *Filipinas Saudi 1*.

Jun 9: In tow for Kaohsiung for breaking up, began to take in water, apparently through various insecure fastenings. Listed and sank in position 07°35′N—60°12′E.

Pasteur 5/157
1985 Feb 12: On voyage Singapore-Madras with 702 passengers fire broke out in after dormitory and spread. 40 lives lost.
Feb 14: Arrived at Madras where laid up.
Apr 8: Arrived at Bombay. Sold to Indian breakers, as *Chidambaram*.

Patria 4/44
1985 Renamed *Aniva*. Sold to Pakistani breakers.

Pendennis Castle 5/113
1976 Aug 9: Laid up at Hong Kong.
1977 To Kinvara Bay Shipping Ltd, Panama. Renamed *Sindbad*, then *Sindbad 1*. Remained laid up.
1980 Apr: To shipbreakers at Kaohsiung.

1

Potsdam 3/224
1976 Feb 20: Arrived at Karachi for last time.
Oct: As *Safina-E-Hujjaj* breaking up commenced by Cheminex Impex, Gadani Beach.

President Adams 4/226
1980 To Cape Cod as training ship *Bay State* for Massachusetts Marine Academy.
1981 Dec 22: Engine-room fire. Badly damaged.
1982 Following commencement of reinstatement work it was established that repairs not justified. Towed to James River. Broken up.

President Wilson 4/154
1976 To Oceanic Cruise Development Inc. Remained laid up.
1984 As *Oriental Empress* broken up by Loy Kee Shipbreakers, Hong Kong.

Rangitane 4/210
1976 Apr 2: As *Oriental Esmeralda* arrived at Kaohsiung where broken up by I Shing Steel & Iron Works.

Rangitoto 4/208
1975 Mar 7: Laid up at Hong Kong.
1976 Feb: As *Oriental Carnaval* breaking up commenced by Lee Sing Shipbreaking Co, Hong Kong.

Rio Tunuyan 4/206
1977 Feb 11: Breaking up commenced by MEM, San Pedro.

Ru Yung 5/134
1982 Jan: Laid up in Taiwan. Broken up same year.

San Jorge 4/48
1981 Broken up at Gadani Beach.

Uganda 5/34
1982 Falklands war. *Uganda* requisitioned by British Government for service as hospital ship.
Aug 9: Arrived Southampton at conclusion of service. Partially refitted for return to cruising.
1983 Jan: Taken over by Ministry of Defence for two years, Ascension-Falkland Islands service.

1985 Apr 25: Laid up in River Fal.
1986 May: Sold to Taiwan breakers. On arrival renamed *Triton*.
Aug: Grounded during typhoon. Turned over on her side. Understood that breaking up proceeded.

Uige 5/83
1978 Nov 29: Sold to Baptista & Irmãos Ltda, Lisbon, for breaking up.
1980 Jul 2: Breaking up commenced.

Vasari 1/60
1979 Feb: As *Pishchevaya Industriya* arrived at Kaohsiung where broken up.

Yapeyú 5/32
1980 Apr 11: As *Iran Cremona* left Malalag Bay for Kaohsiung where broken up.

1 *The* Riviera, *ex* Varna, *ex* Ocean Monarch. (Steffen Weirauch.)
2 *Renamed* Aniva, *the* Rossiya, *ex* Patria, *was sold to breakers in 1985.* (Michael D.J. Lennon.)

2

Bibliography

Material for the ship biographies subsequent to 1976 has been taken from the following publications and periodicals. For sources used in the compilation of the biographies up to that date, see the bibliographies in *Great Passenger Ships of the World, Volumes 1-5*.

Courrier de la Compagnie Générale Maritime, Paris, 1975-1986
Fairplay, London, 1974-1986
Ferry & Ro-ro Guide (formerly *European Ferry List*), Halmstadt, 1977-1986
Germanischer Lloyd, Register, Hamburg, 1984-1986
Hansa, Hamburg, 1974-86
Lloyd's Register of Shipping, London, 1974-1986
Marine News, Kendal, 1974-1986
The Motor Ship, London, 1974-1986
Ocean Cruise News, Stamford, Conn, 1981-1986
Schiff und Hafen, Hamburg, 1974-1986
Schiffahrt international, Herford, 1974-1986
Sea Breezes, Liverpool, 1974-1986
Seewirtschaft, Berlin, 1976-1986
Ships Monthly, Burton-on-Trent, 1974-1986
Ships of the World, Tokyo, 1974-1986
Steamboat Bill, New York, 1974-1986

Public announcements, press reports and the annual reports of shipping companies and shipbuilders have also been referred to.

Errata to Volumes 1-5

VOLUME 1

Page 146 Chicago
Column 1, line 19: After 1929 insert 'Renamed *Guadeloupe*'

Page 180 Titanic
Column 3, line 8: For 'The look-outs were doubled', read 'The look-outs, two as usual, were in the crow's nest'.

Page 182 Titanic
Column 1, line 5: For 'south', read 'north'.
Column 1, line 43: For '30-foot', read '300-foot'.
Column 2, line 21: For '*Burma*', read '*Birma*'.
Column 3, line 18: For '00.45 hrs', read '00.25 hrs'.

Page 184 Titanic
Column 2, line 5: For '41° 16′′ N′, read '41° 46′ N′.

VOLUME 2

Page 12 Bismarck
Column 2, line 8: Delete 'she was then taken round to Liverpool'.

Page 94 Pittsburgh
Line 38: After 1940 insert 'May'.
Line 41: After 1941 insert 'Apr 25'.

VOLUME 3

Page 110 Highland Chieftain
Caption, line 3: For '1950' read '1960'.

Page 166 Empress of Britain
Line 18: For 'Bound from Canada', read 'Bound from Egypt'.

Page 176 Reina del Pacifico
Column 1, line 3: For 'Govan' read 'Belfast'.

Page 210 Normandie
Caption, line 1: For 'entering', read 'leaving'.

Page 220 Abosso
Line 17: For 'went down with the entire crew of 168', read 'went down with nearly all those aboard. Just one lifeboat managed to get away, with 31 survivors including 14 crew members'.

Page 222 Orcades
Line 30: For last four sentences, read 'Two hrs after the first attack she was struck by another three torpedoes, rolled over on her starboard side and sank in position 31° 51′ S – 14° 40′ E. The survivors were picked up by the Polish steamer *Narvik*, which had already picked up those who took to the boats following the first attack. A total of 48 people died in the torpedo explosions and in an accident while the boats were being lowered.'

VOLUME 4

Page 40 Cilicia
Line 14. Add 'Jul 2: Maiden voyage'.

Page 40 Cadedonia
Line 13: Add 'Apr 24: Maiden voyage'.

Page 50 Stockholm
Line 7: For '63.3 ft', read '83.3 ft'.

Page 60 Oranje
Column 1, Line 10: For 'twin screw', read 'triple screw'.

Page 84 America
Column 2, line 5: For '*Westpoint*', read '*West Point*'.

Page 90 Biloxi
Line 12: Add '1943'.

VOLUME 5

Page 111 Santa Rosa
Column 2, line 15: Delete 'Renamed *Samos Sky*. South America service'.

Page 118 Argentina
Column 3, line 11: Delete 'and renamed *Edam*'.

Index of Ships' Names